The Pendulum and Subconscious Communication

Rory Sheehan, B.A., B.Ed., M.B.A.

© 2020, Rory Sheehan

All rights reserved. This book may not be reproduced in whole or in part, stored in a retrieval system, or transmitted in any form or by any means, electronic, mechanical, photocopying, recording, or other without written permission from the publisher.

Published by: PRS Creative Publishing and Productions Inc.

www.positivestrategies.com

Printed in Canada

2020

Disclaimer: The techniques and ideas presented in this book are presented for information purposes only. They are not intended to replace professional opinions for your specific situations. Should you choose to use any of the techniques or ideas presented, you accept full personal responsibility for your choice and will not hold the author, publisher, affiliated companies or families responsible for your decision. You accept that you use these techniques at your own risk.

4 The Pendulum

Contents

About the author	7
Get the most from this book	11
Commonly asked questions	15
Before Your Begin	21
Pendulum Basics	27
Using Pendulum Charts	31
Introductory Steps	37
Pendulum Exercise	41
Yes or No Answers	47
Communication With Your Higher Conscious Mind	59
Subconscious Connection with a Specific Body Part	77
Scale or Range	95
Specific Uses For the Pendulum	113
Using Your Pendulum To Identify Nutritional Deficiencies	115
Using Your Pendulum to Increase Your Energy Level	131

Using Your Pendulum to Relax	149
Using Your Pendulum to Send Healing Energy to a Specific Body Part	167
Using Your Pendulum To Create a Vibrational Alignment with Money	181
Using Your Pendulum to Let Go of a Negative Emotion	195
Using Your Pendulum to Improve the Law of Attraction	211
Communication with your Spirit Guides	227
Pendulum Charts	247
21 Day Challenge	265

About the Author

Rory Sheehan is an entrepreneur committed to helping others succeed in their businesses and personal lives. Through his training programs and speaking engagements, Rory is touching the lives of thousands of people every year. His entertaining and informative sessions have made Rory a trainer in high demand.

Academically, Rory has an Undergraduate Degree from the University of Toronto, a Bachelors of Education Degree from Brock University, and a Masters in Business Administration Degree from Concordia University.

As part of his ongoing research to understand human behaviour and personal excellence, Rory has acquired significant qualifications recognized around the world, including:

- Certification as a Hypnotherapist by the National Guild of Hypnotists.
- Certified as an Instructor of Basic and Advanced Hypnotherapy by the National Guild of Hypnotists.

- Certified as a Master Hypnotist by the American Board of Hypnotherapy.
- Certified as a Hypnotherapist by the American Board of Hypnotherapy.
- Certified as a Practitioner and Master Practitioner of Neuro Linguistic Programming (NLP) by the American Board of Neuro Linguistic Programming.
- Certified as a Practitioner and Master Practitioner of Time Line Therapy™ by the Time Line Therapy Association.
- Attuned as a Reiki Master under the Usui Shiki Ryoho System.

As a television writer, producer, and host, Rory has been fortunate to take his empowering messages to a larger audience with a variety of self-improvement and public interest shows that have been televised across the Province of Ontario.

Many articles that Rory has written have been published in magazines and newspapers. The feedback has been tremendous. Readers like Rory's casual style of writing and the way he presents his ideas in practical and easy to understand language.

Over the past several years Rory Sheehan has become a much sought after speaker and trainer. Rory has conducted small and large group trainings for business people, entrepreneurs, students, and educators. Rory has developed a reputation as a trainer and speaker "who makes a difference".

For more information, on upcoming seminars and workshops, or to book your training with Rory, contact Positive Strategies at (905) 231-0884 or through their WEB site at
www.positivestrategies.com

10 The Pendulum

Get The Most From This Book

How To Get The Most From This Book

This book is intended to be used as a manual to help you better understand how to use a Pendulum as a communication tool. We will be looking at the Pendulum as a way for you to communicate with your Subconscious Mind, Your Higher Conscious Mind, and different Body Parts.

We will also cover how the Pendulum can be used to change your Vibrational Frequency, provide Healing Energy, and Reduce Stress.

As you work through the information presented, you will develop a better understanding of the Pendulum and all the benefits available to you,

The section on Practical Applications for the Pendulum will guide you step by step through a series of uses for the Pendulum. Each one is set up so it is self-contained. There will be no flipping pages or trying to remember what to do, because each application includes all the steps.

14 The Pendulum

The more you practice using your Pendulum, the easier it will be to use, and the more powerful the Pendulum will become as a communication tool.

Enjoy learning about the Pendulum and remember to practice often.

The Pendulum 15

Commonly Asked Questions

Commonly Asked Questions

What is a pendulum?

A pendulum is simply a weight, held at the end of a string or chain, where the weight can swing freely as you hold the other end of the string or chain with your fingers.

What do we use a pendulum for?

We use the pendulum as a tool to communicate with our subconscious mind, higher conscious, and Spirit Guides. We can use the pendulum to get answers to important questions, to relax, and to help change our emotional state. The pendulum has also helpful at sending healing energy to specific body parts.

How does a pendulum work?

Our subconscious mind moves the muscles that control the pendulum. In this way, we are able to benefit from information received directly from our subconscious mind.

Can everyone benefit from using a pendulum?

Yes, with some training, and a little practice, everyone can benefit from using a pendulum.

Can children benefit from using a pendulum?

Yes, but children need to be supervised to unsure that they are using the pendulum properly and not as a toy or game.

Is it difficult to use a pendulum?

No, a pendulum is a very powerful tool that can be mastered with some instruction and practice.

Is a pendulum always right?

The pendulum will always answer your exact question, so be very careful how you word the question. When formulating your question, ask yourself if a five year old child could understand and be able to answer this question. If not, then the question needs to be changed.

What can I do if I don't like the answer I receive?

If you receive an answer you do not like, you should ask for clarification to make sure you are interpreting the answer correctly.
An example of a clarifying question would be to ask your pendulum:
When you say _____, do you mean _____?

Then you should ask for guidance to help you move in the direction you want to move. An example of a guidance question would be to ask your pendulum:
Would it be helpful if I ___?

Is one type of pendulum more effective than another?

Choosing a pendulum is a matter of personal preference. You may find yourself drawn to a specific pendulum, and that would make it the most appropriate pendulum for you. If you do not feel drawn to any specific pendulum, then any weight at the end of a string or chain will work fine.

Will the pendulum still work if I am really nervous?

It is always best to relax as much as possible before you start working with your pendulum. If you are really nervous, your hands may tremble, even a little, and that will interfere with the information you are seeking.

Can I let someone else use my pendulum?

Ideally you want to create an energy connection between you and your pendulum. Therefore, no one else should use, or even touch your pendulum, because it will change the energy connection.

Do I have to program the pendulum every time I use it?

Yes, it is very important that you program your pendulum before every use. This makes sure that you are always clear in the directions that are being used.

Do I have to energize the pendulum everything I use it?

Although your pendulum will take on more and more of your energy the more you interact with it, it is always a good idea to take a moment before you use your pendulum to make sure your energy is in line.

Is it okay to allow the pendulum to choose the meaning for each direction?

No, it is very important that you choose the meaning for each direction. You need to program your pendulum, so it is clear what each direction means. The subconscious mind is like a five year old child and this means that you need to make sure that you are in charge and that your subconscious will do what you ask it to do.

Before You Begin

Before You Start Using Your Pendulum

This Chapter will give you some information on choosing the right Pendulum for you and what needs to be done to your Pendulum to get it ready for you to use it as a communication tool.

Choose the Right Pendulum

Choosing a pendulum is a very personal experience. Time and care should be taken to make sure you feel right about your choice. Trust your intuition.

Be sure that your pendulum swings comfortably and is comfortable in your hand while you hold it.

Clear the Pendulum

Clearing your pendulum will clear any unwanted energy that may be attached to the pendulum.

Here are some options for clearing your pendulum:

- Bury the pendulum in a pot of soil overnight and allow the energy of the earth to clear any negative energy from the pendulum.
- Hold the pendulum under running water for approximately 60 seconds to allow the purity of the water to clear any negative energy from the pendulum.
- Hold the pendulum in your hands for approximately three minutes as you imagine any negative energy leaving the pendulum and you imagine yourself physically throwing that negative energy away.

Remember to make sure that your pendulum has been cleared of any negative energies before and after each use.

Energize your Pendulum

Your pendulum needs to be attuned to your personal energy. This means that you need to create a strong energy connection between you and your pendulum.

Some examples to help you create this strong connection and to energize your pendulum include:
- Hold your pendulum between your palms and imagine positive energy moving from you to your pendulum. You can imagine this positive energy in the form of sunlight shining on your pendulum. This should be done for approximately three minutes.

- Wear your pendulum on a chain around your neck and carry it with you so that your pendulum can feel your energy over a period of time. This may take a few days before you can feel comfortable using your pendulum for the first time.

- Place your pendulum under your pillow so it can absorb your energy while you sleep.

After you have removed all negative energy that may have been connected to the Pendulum, and given the pendulum your positive energy, you have now made the Pendulum your own.

Once you feel comfortable with the energy of the Pendulum, you are ready to move forward and start to build rapport with your Pendulum.

The Pendulum 27

Pendulum Basics

Basics for Using Your Pendulum

Holding the Pendulum

The string or chain of your Pendulum should be held with the thumb and forefinger of the hand that you write with. There should be about three or four inches of string or chain between your fingers and your pendulum.

Your arms should be up and not resting on anything. Your feet should be flat on the floor and your back should be supported.

Relax

Take a deep breath and allow yourself to relax. You will find that your pendulum will move much more freely if you are relaxed and free from tension.

If it takes a few minutes to get yourself into the right frame of mind to use your pendulum, that is fine. Simply focus on your breathing and allowing yourself to relax until you are ready to use your pendulum.

Using Your Pendulum for the First Time

Now that you are relaxed, you are ready to use your pendulum for the first time.

Hold the string, or chain, of your pendulum between the thumb and fore finger of the hand that you write with. Focus all your attention on your pendulum. Stare at your pendulum. Concentrate on your pendulum. Now, using your thoughts, and only your thoughts, tell your pendulum to move from side to side. Hold this focus until you notice your pendulum start to move.

Once you are successful at getting your Pendulum to move from side to side, then using your thoughts and only your thoughts, tell your pendulum to slow down and stop. Hold this focus until your pendulum stops moving.

Once your pendulum stops moving, tell your pendulum, using your thoughts and only your

thoughts, to move forwards and back.
Hold this focus until you notice your
pendulum start to move.

Now, tell your pendulum to move in a
circle, around and around in a nice, easy to
see, circle.

Hold this focus until you notice your
pendulum start to move in a circle.

Now, using your thoughts and only your
thoughts, tell your pendulum to slow
down and stop. Hold this focus until your
pendulum stops moving.

Once you have successfully moved the
pendulum in these three directions, you
are ready to start using your pendulum for
communication and information
purposes.

Using Pendulum Charts

Pendulum Charts

Practice Pendulum Chart

Your Practice Pendulum Chart is intended for you to get more comfortable with using your Pendulum as well as to help you build a strong rapport with your Pendulum as a communication tool.

Start by using your thoughts to direct your Pendulum to move along one of the lines in your Practice Pendulum Chart. Continue to work with your Practice Pendulum Chart until you are comfortable directing your Pendulum to move along each of the lines in the Practice Pendulum Chart.

The Yes or No Chart

We will use the **Yes or No Chart** whenever we want to ask questions where the answer will be either "Yes", or "No".

Take a minute to look at the **Yes or No Chart** before you start to use it. Notice that there are specific directions for each response you will receive from your pendulum.

The direction that represents **Yes** is forwards and back, just as you would nod your head to say yes.

The direction that represents **No** is side to side, just as you would shake your head to say no.

The direction that represents **Maybe** is a diagonal from top left to bottom right.

The direction that represents **Rephrase Question,** which means that your questions was not clear and needs to be asked again in a different way, is a diagonal from top right to bottom left.

We will always be using these directions whenever we use the **Yes or No Chart.**

Asking Yes or No Questions

To ask a question that will lead to an answer of Yes or No, simply word your question starting with any word other than: who, what, where, when, how, or why.

Examples of Yes or No questions include:
- *Do I need ... ?*
- *Can I ... ?*
- *Is it a good idea to ... ?*
- *Would it be best to ... ?*
- *Does ... make sense?*

The Scale or Range Chart

We will use the **Range Chart** in a number of different ways. These different ways include:
- Increasing energy from low to high
- Decreasing stress from high to low
- Identifying our current energy level based on a range we define

There are a number of different Scale or Range Pendulum Charts provided in the back of the book. Please feel free to make up your own Range Chart for anything specific situation you feel would be beneficial to you.

Introductory Steps

Each Time You Use Your Pendulum

The following steps should be completed before you use your pendulum. It is best that you don't skip any of the steps and that you work through each of these steps every time you use your pendulum.

Get Emotionally Ready

Your pendulum will take on your emotional energy, so it is very important that you are in a positive emotional state and feeling relaxed whenever you use your pendulum.

Breathe easy and allow yourself to relax before you begin using your pendulum.

Get Mentally Ready

Take a deep breath and allow yourself to relax. Clear your mind of all chatter and focus all your attention on the Pendulum exercise you are about to work through. The more mentally relaxed you feel while using your Pendulum, the stronger the results you will experience.

Get Physically Ready

Find a comfortable place where you feel relaxed and at ease. Ideally, you should sit up

straight, with both feet flat on the floor. Hold the string or chain of your pendulum between your thumb and forefinger of the hand that you write with. There should be at least 2 or 3 inches between your fingers and the pendulum. Be sure that your arm and elbow are not resting on anything.

Focus Your Energy

All of your attention and energy should be focused on your pendulum. Any pendulum chart that you are using should be observed through your peripheral vision as you hold your full attention on your pendulum.

Set Your Intention

Be very clear on what outcome you hope to achieve by using your pendulum. You also want to make it clear that your intention is to only receive guidance that is for your highest and best good.

An example would be to hold your pendulum as you say: ***My intention with this exercise is to receive truthful answers which will serve the positive and higher purpose of everyone involved.***

Program Your Pendulum

It is very important to take the time to program your Pendulum before every use. The subconscious mind is like a five year old child, and sometimes it does not want to communicate in the exact way you expect. Because of this, it is important to program your pendulum before each use to make sure that you and your subconscious mind are in alignment.

There are specific programing instructions provided in the book for each method of communication using your pendulum.

Pendulum Exercises

Pendulum Exercises

Use the ***Practice Pendulum Chart*** for each of the following Pendulum Exercises.

Exercise 1: Side to side between 1 and 2

Hold your pendulum above the center spot. Using your thoughts and only your thoughts, direct the pendulum to move side to side between 1 and 2.

You should practice this exercise until the pendulum moves freely between 1 and 2. Your pendulum should move enough so that it is very clear that the movement is between 1 and 2.

Exercise 2: Forwards and back between 3 and 4

Hold your pendulum above the center spot. Using your thoughts and only your thoughts, direct the pendulum to move forwards and back between 3 and 4.

You should practice this exercise until the pendulum moves freely between 3 and 4. Your pendulum should move enough so that it is very clear that the movement is between 3 and 4.

Exercise 3: On an angle between 5 and 6

Hold your pendulum above the center spot. Using your thoughts and only your thoughts, direct the pendulum to move on an angle between 5 and 6.

You should practice this exercise until the pendulum moves freely on an angle between 5 and 6. Your pendulum should move enough so that it is very clear that the movement is between 5 and 6.

Exercise 4: On an angle between 7 and 8

Hold your pendulum above the center spot. Using your thoughts and only your thoughts, direct the pendulum to move on an angle between 7 and 8.

You should practice this exercise until the pendulum moves freely on an angle between 7 and 8. Your pendulum should move enough so that it is very clear that the movement is between 7 and 8.

Exercise 5: Clockwise

Hold your pendulum above the center spot. Using your thoughts and only your thoughts, direct the pendulum to move clockwise, in a nice, big, and easy to see circle.

You should practice this exercise until the pendulum moves clockwise in a nice big easy to see circle. Your pendulum should move enough so that it is very clear that the movement is clockwise in a circle.

Exercise 6: Counter Clockwise

Hold your pendulum above the center spot. Using your thoughts and only your thoughts, direct the pendulum to move counter clockwise, in a nice, big, and easy to see circle.

You should practice this exercise until the pendulum moves counter clockwise in a nice big easy to see circle. Your pendulum should move enough so that it is very clear that the movement is counter clockwise in a circle.

The Pendulum 45

Yes or No Answers

How to Use Your Pendulum to receive
Yes or No Answers from Your Subconscious Mind

In this section we will use the Pendulum to get information that requires a specific Yes or No answer. You will be communicating with your subconscious mind.

The **Yes or No Pendulum Chart** at the back of this book will help with Yes or No answers.

1- Get Emotionally Ready

Your pendulum will take on your emotional energy, so it is very important that you are in a positive emotional state and feeling relaxed whenever you use your pendulum.

Breathe easy and allow yourself to relax before you begin using your pendulum.

2- Get Mentally Ready

Take a deep breath and allow yourself to relax. Clear your mind of all chatter and focus all your attention on the Pendulum exercise you are about to work through. The more mentally relaxed you feel while using your Pendulum, the stronger the results you will experience.

3- Get Physically Ready

Find a comfortable place where you feel relaxed and at ease. Ideally, you should sit up straight, with both feet flat on the floor. Hold the string or chain of your pendulum between your thumb and forefinger of the hand that you write with. There should be at least 2 or 3 inches between your fingers and the pendulum. Be sure that your arm and elbow are not resting on anything.

4- Focus Your Energy

All your attention and energy should be focused on your pendulum. Any pendulum chart that you are using should be observed through your peripheral vision as you hold your full attention on your pendulum.

5- Set Your Intention

Be very clear on what outcome you hope to achieve by using your Pendulum. You also want to make it

clear that your intention is to only receive guidance that is for your highest and best good.

An example would be to hold your pendulum as you say: ***My intention with this exercise is to receive truthful answers which will serve the positive and higher purpose of everyone involved.***

6- Connecting with Your Subconscious Mind

Using a pendulum all starts with a strong and positive connection with your subconscious mind.

To do this, take a deep breath and allow yourself to relax. Ask your pendulum to move side to side as an indication that you are connected to your subconscious mind.

7- Program Your Pendulum for the Subconscious Mind

Once your pendulum starts to move, and a connection with your subconscious mind has been established, you need to program your pendulum to communicate with your subconscious mind.

Follow these steps to program your pendulum for communication with your subconscious mind:

- Hold your pendulum so that it is hanging about two inches above the direct center of your **Yes or No Pendulum Chart**.

- To train your Pendulum and your subconscious mind to both understand the direction that represents Yes, swing the pendulum forwards and back as you repeat the following statement three times:
  *This is the direction to represent **Yes** with my subconscious mind. (3 times)*

- To train your Pendulum and your subconscious mind to both understand the direction that represents No, swing the pendulum from left to right as you repeat three times:

*This is the direction to represent **No** with my subconscious mind. (3 times)*

- To train your Pendulum and your subconscious mind to both understand the direction that represents Maybe, swing the pendulum on an angle from top right to bottom left as you repeat three times:
  *This is the direction to represent **Maybe** with my subconscious mind. (3 times)*

- To train your Pendulum and your subconscious mind to both understand the direction that represents Rephrase Question, swing the Pendulum on an angle from top left to bottom right as you repeat three times:
  *This is the direction to represent **Rephrase Question** with my subconscious mind. (3 times)*

8- Test the Programing

At this point you want to test that your

subconscious mind has accepted the directions you have just programmed using your Pendulum. This testing will be a two-step process.

The first step in testing your pendulum is to focus all your attention on the pendulum as you repeat the following statements one at a time:

- *Show me the direction that represents **yes**.*
  Stay focused on this statement until your pendulum moves in the direction that represents Yes. If your pendulum should move in any other direction, then you must take the time to go back and program your pendulum again.

- *Show me the direction that represents **No**.*
  Stay focused on this statement until your pendulum moves in the direction that represents No. If your pendulum should move in any other direction, then you must take the time to go back and program your pendulum again.

- *Show me the direction that represents **Maybe**.*

    Stay focused on this statement until your pendulum moves in the direction that represents maybe. If your pendulum should move in any other direction, then you must take the time to go back and program your pendulum again.

- *Show me the direction that represents **Rephrase Question**.*

    Stay focused on this statement until your pendulum moves in the direction that represents Rephrase Question. If your pendulum should move in any other direction, then you must take the time to go back and program your pendulum again.

In the second step to test the programming of your pendulum, you will ask your pendulum a series of **Yes or No** questions that you already know the answers to.

Examples of possible testing questions may include:

- *Is my name _____?*
- *Is my address _____?*
- *Is my age _____?*

Your objective with this test is to make sure that "**Yes**" **is yes,** and **"No" is no**.

If any of the answers you receive are incorrect, go back and repeat the programing of Yes and No until the test works out positively.

9- Subconscious Commitment

You want a commitment from your subconscious mind that it is willing to work with you to achieve the best possible results with your pendulum.

To establish a subconscious commitment, ask your pendulum the following questions:
- *My intention with using this pendulum is to help myself in a positive and healthy way. Does my subconscious mind understand my positive intention?*

- *To achieve the best possible results with the pendulum I need the full cooperation of my subconscious mind. Is my subconscious mind willing to work with me to achieve the best possible results?*

Only continue if your subconscious mind responds "Yes" to each of these questions. If you receive a "No" answer, you should take a break and return some other time to work with your pendulum.

10- Asking Yes or No Questions

Questions should be clear and understandable and should always lead to a Yes or No answer. Questions should only be about you.

Be sure that your Pendulum comes to a complete stop between each question so that nothing can influence the answer to the next question.

If the Pendulum is not moving enough to receive a clear answer, ask your pendulum to show you a clearer and easier to see answer.

11- Clear the Pendulum

After you have received an answer to your specific question it is important that you **clear your pendulum** so that it is clear that you are finished with that question and you are ready to move on to the next question.

To clear your pendulum, simply hold the weight of your pendulum in the palm of your other hand. This will relax the energy in your pendulum and allow it to prepare for the next question.

12- Say Thank You to Your Pendulum

While you are holding the weight of your Pendulum in your hands, say *thank you to your Pendulum for allowing you to experience all the benefits of the exercise.* .

13- Saying Thank You to Subconscious Mind

It is important to say thank you after you receive an answer to each of your questions. This will keep you in a positive frame of mind where the focus is gratitude.

It is also important to say thank you for all the guidance you have received when you have finished asking all your questions and you are about to end the session with your pendulum.

14- Back to Full Awareness

After you say thank you to your subconscious mind, you can take a deep breath and bring yourself back to full awareness.

Communication With Your Higher Conscious Mind

Using the Pendulum to get Yes or No answers While Communicating with Your Higher Conscious

In this section we will use the pendulum to get information that requires a specific **Yes** or **No** answer from our Higher Conscious. This higher connection may be: Your Higher Conscious Mind, Your Guardian Angel, or one of Your Spirit Guides. It is up to you to decide who you want to communicate with in each specific session with your Pendulum.

The **Yes or No Pendulum Chart** will help with **Yes** or **No** answers.

1- Get Emotionally Ready

Your pendulum will take on your emotional energy, so it is very important that you are in a positive emotional state and feeling relaxed whenever you use your pendulum.

Breathe easy and allow yourself to relax before you begin using your pendulum.

2- Get Mentally Ready

Take a deep breath and allow yourself to relax. Clear your mind of all chatter and focus all your attention on the Pendulum exercise you are about to work through. The more mentally relaxed you feel while using your Pendulum, the stronger the results you will experience.

3- Get Physically Ready

Find a comfortable place where you feel relaxed and at ease. Ideally, you should sit up straight, with both feet flat on the floor. Hold the string or chain of your pendulum between your thumb and forefinger of the hand that you write with. There should be at least 2 or 3 inches between your fingers and the pendulum. Be sure that your arm and elbow are not resting on anything.

4- Focus Your Energy

All your attention and energy should be focused on your pendulum. Any pendulum chart that you are using should be observed through your peripheral vision as you hold your full attention on your pendulum.

5- Set Your Intention

Be very clear on what outcome you hope to achieve by using your Pendulum. You also want to make it clear that your intention is to only receive guidance that is for your highest and best good.

An example would be to hold your pendulum as you say: ***My intention with this exercise is to receive truthful answers which will serve the positive and higher purpose of everyone involved.***

6- Connecting with Your Subconscious Mind

Using a pendulum all starts with a strong and positive connection with your subconscious mind.

To do this, take a deep breath and allow yourself to relax. Ask your pendulum to move side to side as an indication that you are connected to your subconscious mind.

7. Program Your Pendulum for the Subconscious Mind

Once a connection with your subconscious mind has been established, you need to program your pendulum to communicate with your subconscious mind.

Follow these steps to program your pendulum for communication with your subconscious mind:

- Hold your pendulum so that it is hanging about two inches above the direct center of your **Yes or No Pendulum Chart**.

- To train your Pendulum and your subconscious mind to both understand the direction that represents Yes, swing the pendulum forwards and back as you repeat the following statement three times:
*This is the direction to represent **Yes** with my subconscious mind. (3 times)*

- To train your Pendulum and your subconscious mind to both understand the direction that

The Pendulum 63

represents No, swing the

- pendulum from left to right as you repeat three times:
  *This is the direction to represent **No** with my subconscious mind. (3 times)*

- To train your Pendulum and your subconscious mind to both understand the direction that represents Maybe, swing the pendulum on an angle from top right to bottom left as you repeat three times:
  *This is the direction to represent **Maybe** with my subconscious mind. (3 times)*

- To train your Pendulum and your subconscious mind to both understand the direction that represents Rephrase Question, swing the Pendulum on an angle from top left to bottom right as you repeat three times:
  *This is the direction to represent **Rephrase Question** with my subconscious mind. (3 times)*

8- Test the Programing

At this point you want to test that your subconscious mind has accepted the directions you have just programmed using your pendulum. This testing will be a two-step process.

The first step in testing your pendulum is to focus all your attention on the pendulum as you repeat the following statements one at a time:

- *Show me the direction that represents **yes**.*

Stay focused on this statement until your pendulum moves in the direction that represents yes. If your pendulum should move in any other direction, then you must take the time to go back and program your pendulum again.

- *Show me the direction that represents **no**.*

Stay focused on this statement until your pendulum moves in the direction that represents no. If your pendulum should move in any other direction, then you must take the time to go back and program your pendulum again.

- *Show me the direction that represents **maybe**.*

    Stay focused on this statement until your pendulum moves in the direction that represents maybe. If your pendulum should move in any other direction, then you must take the time to go back and program your pendulum again.

- *Show me the direction that represents **not sure**.*

    Stay focused on this statement until your pendulum moves in the direction that represents not sure. If your pendulum should move in any other direction, then you must take the time to go back and program your pendulum again.

In the second step to testing your pendulum, you will ask your pendulum a series of **yes** or **no** questions that you already know the answers to.

Examples of possible testing questions may include:

- *Is my name _____?*
- *Is my address _____?*
- *Is my age _____?*

Your objective with this test is to make sure that **yes** is yes, and **no** is no.

If the signals are not coming out right, go back and repeat the programing of **yes** and **no** until the test works out positively.

9- Subconscious Commitment

You want a commitment from your subconscious mind that it is willing to work with you to achieve the best possible results with your pendulum.

To establish a subconscious commitment, ask your pendulum the following questions:

- *My intention with using this pendulum is to help myself in a positive and healthy way. Does my subconscious mind understand my positive intention?*

- *To achieve the best possible results with the pendulum I need the full cooperation of my subconscious mind. Is my subconscious mind willing to work with me to achieve the best possible results?*

Only continue if your subconscious mind responds "Yes" to each of these questions. If you receive a "No" answer, you should take a break and return some other time to work with your pendulum.

10- Connecting with the Higher Conscious

At this point we want to move from a connection with the subconscious mind to a higher connection. This higher connection may be: Your Higher Conscious Mind, Your Guardian Angel, one of Your Spirit Guides.

The steps here are similar to the steps you took when you connected with your subconscious mind.

To connect with your Higher Conscious, continue to breathe easily, and allow yourself to relax even more. Ask your pendulum to move in some way as an indication you are connected to your Higher Conscious.

11- Program Your Pendulum for Communication with your Higher Conscious

Once your pendulum has moved to indicate a connection with your Higher Conscious, you need to program your pendulum to communicate with your Higher Conscious.

Follow these steps to program your pendulum for communication with your Higher Conscious:

- Hold your pendulum so that it is hanging about two inches above the direct center of your **Yes or No Pendulum Chart**.

- To train your Pendulum and your Higher Conscious Mind to both understand the direction that represents Yes, swing the pendulum forwards and back as you repeat the following statement three times:

70 The Pendulum

*This is the direction to represent **Yes** with my Higher Conscious Mind. (3 times)*

- To train your Pendulum and your Higher Conscious Mind to both understand the direction that represents No, swing the pendulum from left to right as you repeat three times:
  *This is the direction to represent **No** with my Higher Conscious Mind. (3 times)*

- To train your Pendulum and your Higher Conscious Mind to both understand the direction that represents Maybe, swing the pendulum on an angle from top right to bottom left as you repeat three times:
  *This is the direction to represent **Maybe** with my Higher Conscious Mind. (3 times)*

- To train your Pendulum and your Higher Conscious Mind to both understand the direction that represents Rephrase Question, swing the Pendulum on an angle from top left to bottom right as you

- repeat three times:
*This is the direction to represent **Rephrase Question** with my Higher Conscious Mind. (3 times)*

12- Test the Programing

At this point you want to test that your Higher Conscious has accepted the programing for Yes and No. To test this, you simply need to ask your pendulum a series of yes and no questions that you already know the answers for, just as you did with testing the subconscious mind.

Examples of possible testing questions may include:

- *Is my name _____?*
- *Is my address _____?*
- *Are my eyes the colour _____?*

Be sure to ask questions where you know with certainty that the answers are **yes** and other questions where you know with certainty that the answers are **no**.

Your objective with this test is to make sure that **"Yes"** is yes, and **"No"** is no.

If the signals are not coming out right, go back and repeat the programing of Yes and No for connecting with your Higher Conscious Mind until the test works out positively.

13- Higher Conscious Commitment

You want a commitment from your Higher Conscious that it is willing to work with you to achieve the best possible results with your pendulum.

To establish this Higher Conscious commitment, ask your pendulum the following questions:

- *My intention with using this pendulum is to help myself in a positive and healthy way. Does my Higher Conscious understand my positive intention?*

- *To achieve the best possible results with the pendulum I need the full cooperation of my Higher Conscious. Is my Higher Conscious willing to work with me to achieve the best possible results?*

Only continue if your Higher Conscious responds **yes** to each of these questions. If you received a **no** to any of these questions, say thank you to your Higher Conscious and take a break. You can return and work with your pendulum at another time.

14- Asking Yes or No Questions

Questions should be clear and understandable and should always lead to a **yes** or **no** answer. Questions should only be about you.

Be sure that your pendulum comes to a complete stop between questions so that nothing can influence the answer to the next question.

If the answer is not clear, ask your pendulum to show you a more clear and easier to see answer.

15- Say Thank You After Each Answer

It is important to say thank you after you receive an answer to each of your questions. This will keep you in a positive frame of mind where the focus is gratitude.

16- Clear the Pendulum

After you have received an answer to your specific question it is important that you **clear your pendulum** so that it is understood that you are finished with that question and you are ready to move on to the next question.

To clear your pendulum, simply hold the weight of your pendulum in the palm of your other hand. This will relax the energy in your pendulum and allow it to prepare for the next question.

17- Saying Thank You to Your Higher Conscious

When you feel confident that you have received all the guidance from your Higher Conscious that you need at this time, it is important to say thank you to your Higher Conscious.

76 The Pendulum

18- Saying Thank You to Your Subconscious

After you say thank you to your Higher Conscious, then it is important to say thank you to your subconscious mind.

19- Back to Full Awareness

After you say thank you to your subconscious mind, you can take a deep breath and bring yourself back to full awareness.

Subconscious Connection with a Specific Body Part

Using the Pendulum to get Yes or No Answers From a Specific Body Part

In this section we will use the pendulum to get information that requires a specific **Yes** or **No** answer from a specific body part.

The **Yes or No Pendulum Chart** will help with **yes** or **no** answers.

1- Get Emotionally Ready

Your pendulum will take on your emotional energy, so it is very important that you are in a positive emotional state and feeling relaxed whenever you use your pendulum.

Breathe easy and allow yourself to relax before you begin using your pendulum.

2- Get Mentally Ready

Take a deep breath and allow yourself to relax. Clear your mind of all chatter and focus all your attention on the Pendulum exercise you are about to work through.

80 The Pendulum

The more mentally relaxed you feel while using your Pendulum, the stronger the results you will experience.

3- Get Physically Ready

Find a comfortable place where you feel relaxed and at ease. Ideally, you should sit up straight, with both feet flat on the floor. Hold the string or chain of your pendulum between your thumb and forefinger of the hand that you write with. There should be at least 2 or 3 inches between your fingers and the pendulum. Be sure that your arm and elbow are not resting on anything.

4- Focus Your Energy

All your attention and energy should be focused on your pendulum. Any pendulum chart that you are using should be observed through your peripheral vision as you hold your full attention on your pendulum.

5- Set Your Intention

Be very clear on what outcome you hope to achieve by using your outcome. You also want to make it clear that your intention is to only receive guidance that is for your highest and best good.

An example would be to hold your pendulum as you say:
> *My intention with this exercise is to receive truthful answers which will serve the positive and higher purpose of everyone involved.*

6- Connecting with Your Subconscious Mind

Using a pendulum all starts with a strong and positive connection with your subconscious mind.

To do this, take a deep breath and allow yourself to relax. Ask your pendulum to move side to side as an indication that you are connected to your subconscious mind.

7- Program Your Pendulum for the Subconscious Mind

Once a connection with your subconscious mind has been established, you need to program your pendulum to communicate with your subconscious mind.

Follow these steps to program your pendulum for communication with your subconscious mind:

- Hold your pendulum so that it is hanging about two inches above the direct center of your **Yes or No Pendulum Chart**.

- Swing the pendulum forwards and back as you repeat three times:
    *This is the direction to represent **yes** with my subconscious mind.*

- Swing the pendulum from left to right as you repeat three times:
    *This is the direction to represent **no** with my subconscious mind.*

- Swing the pendulum on an angle from top right to bottom left as you repeat three times:
    *This is the direction to represent **maybe** with my subconscious mind.*

- Swing the pendulum on an angle from top left to bottom right as you repeat three times:
    *This is the direction to represent **not clear** with my subconscious mind.*

8- Test the Programing

At this point you want to test that your subconscious mind has accepted the directions you have just programmed using your pendulum. This testing will be a two-step process.

The first step in testing your pendulum is to focus all your attention on the pendulum as you repeat the following statements one at a time:

- *Show me the direction that represents **yes**.*
  Stay focused on this statement until your pendulum moves in the direction that represents yes.

  If your pendulum should move in any other direction, then you must take the time to go back and program your pendulum again.

- *Show me the direction that represents **no**.*
  Stay focused on this statement until your pendulum moves in the direction that represents no. If your pendulum should move in any other direction, then you must take the time to go back and program your pendulum again.

- *Show me the direction that represents **maybe**.*

Stay focused on this statement until your pendulum moves in the direction that represents maybe. If your pendulum should move in any other direction, then you must take the time to go back and program your pendulum again.

- *Show me the direction that represents **not sure**.*

Stay focused on this statement until your pendulum moves in the direction that represents not sure. If your pendulum should move in any other direction, then you must take the time to go back and program your pendulum again.

In the second step to testing your pendulum, you will ask your pendulum a series of **yes** or **no** questions that you already know the answers to.

Examples of possible testing questions may include:

- *Is my name _____?*
- *Is my address _____?*
- *Is my age _____?*

Your objective with this test is to make sure that **yes** is yes, and **no** is no.
If the signals are not coming out right, go back and repeat the programing of yes and no until the test works out positively.

9- Subconscious Commitment

You want a commitment from your subconscious mind that it is willing to work with you to achieve the best possible results with your pendulum.

To establish a subconscious commitment, ask your pendulum the following questions:

- *My intention with using this pendulum is to help myself in a positive and healthy way. Does my subconscious mind understand my positive intention?*

- *To achieve the best possible results with the pendulum I need the full cooperation of my subconscious mind. Is my subconscious mind willing to work with me to achieve the best possible results?*

Only continue if your subconscious mind responds **yes** to each of these questions.

10- Connecting with a Specific Body Part

At this point we want to move from a connection with the subconscious mind to a connection with a specific body part. Connecting with a specific body part allows us to gather information on how long it will take this body part to heal, is it willing to heal faster, and to provide healing energy directly to that specific body part.

The steps here are similar to the steps you took when you connected with your subconscious mind.

To connect with a specific body part, continue to breathe easily, and allow yourself to relax even more. Ask your pendulum to move in some way as an indication you are connected to the intended specific body part.

11- Program Your Pendulum for Communication with a Specific Body Part

Once your pendulum has moved to indicate a connection with a **specific body part**, you need to program your pendulum to communicate with that **specific body part**.

The Pendulum

Follow these steps to program your pendulum for communication with a **specific body part:**

- Hold your pendulum so that it is hanging about two inches above the direct center of your **Yes or No Pendulum Chart**.

- To train your Pendulum and the specific body part to both understand the direction that represents Yes, swing the pendulum forwards and back as you repeat the following statement three times:
  *This is the direction to represent **Yes** with my specific body part. (3 times)*

- To train your Pendulum and your specific body part to both understand the direction that represents No, swing the pendulum from left to right as you repeat three times:
  *This is the direction to represent **No** with my specific body part. (3 times)*

- To train your Pendulum and your specific body part to both understand the direction that represents Maybe, swing the pendulum on an angle from top right to bottom left as you repeat three times:

The Pendulum 89

*This is the direction to represent **Maybe** with my specific body part. (3 times)*

- To train your Pendulum and your specific body part to both understand the direction that represents Rephrase Question, swing the Pendulum on an angle from top left to bottom right as you repeat three times:
  *This is the direction to represent **Rephrase Question** with my specific body part. (3 times)*

12- Test the Programing

At this point you want to test that a Specific Body Part has accepted the programing for **yes** and **no**. To test this, you simply need to ask your pendulum a series of **yes** and **no** questions that you already know the answers for, just as you did with testing the subconscious mind.

Examples of possible testing questions may include:

- *Does this specific body part recognize my name as _____?*
- *Does this specific body part understand that my address is _____?*
- *Does this specific body part know that my eyes are the colour _____?*

Be sure to ask questions where you know with certainty that the answers are **yes** and other questions where you know with certainty that the answers are **no**.

Your objective with this test is to make sure that **"Yes"** is yes, and **"No"** is no.

If the signals are not coming out right, go back and repeat the programing of **yes** and **no** for a specific body part until the test works out positively.

13- Specific Body Part Commitment

You want a commitment from a Specific Body Part that it is willing to work with you to achieve the best possible results with your pendulum.

To establish a Specific Body Part commitment, ask your pendulum the following questions:

- *My intention with using this pendulum is to help myself in a positive and healthy way. Does this Specific Body Part understand my positive intention?*

- *To achieve the best possible results with the pendulum I need the full cooperation of this Specific Body Part. Is this Specific Body Part willing to work with me to achieve the best possible results?*

    Only continue if the specific body part responds **yes** to each of these questions.

14- Asking Yes or No Questions

Questions should be clear and understandable and should always lead to a **yes** or **no** answer. Questions should only be about you.

Be sure that your pendulum comes to a complete stop between questions so that nothing can influence the answer to the next question.

If the answer is **not clear**, ask your pendulum to show you a clearer and easier to see answer.

15- Saying Thank You After Each Answer

It is important to say *thank you* after you receive an answer to each of your questions. This will keep you in a positive frame of mind where the focus is gratitude.

16- Clear the Pendulum

After you have received an answer to your specific question it is important that you **clear your pendulum** so that it is clear that you are finished with that question and you are ready to move on to the next question.

To clear your pendulum, simply hold the weight of your pendulum in the palm of your other hand. This will relax the energy in your pendulum and allow it to prepare for the next question.

17. Saying Thank You to Your Specific Body Part

When you feel confident that you have received all the guidance from your body part that you need at this time, it is important to say *thank you* to your body part for working with you.

18- Say Thank You to Your Pendulum

While you are holding the weight of your Pendulum in your hands, say *thank you to your Pendulum for allowing you to experience all the benefits of the exercise.* .

19- Saying Thank You to Your Subconscious Mind

After you say *thank you* to your body part, then it is important to say *thank you* to your subconscious mind.

20- Back to Full Awareness

After you say *thank you* to your subconscious mind, you can take a deep breath and bring yourself back to full awareness.

Scale or Range

Using the Pendulum to Work with a Scale or a Range

In this section we will use the pendulum to work with a scale or a range.

The **Scale or Range Pendulum Chart** will help when working with a Scale or a Range.

1- Get Emotionally Ready

Your pendulum will take on your emotional energy, so it is very important that you are in a positive and relaxed emotional state whenever you use your pendulum.

Breathe easy and allow yourself to relax before you begin using your pendulum.

2- Get Mentally Ready

Take a deep breath and allow yourself to relax. Clear your mind of all chatter and focus all your attention on the Pendulum exercise you are about to work through. The more mentally relaxed you feel while using your Pendulum, the stronger the results you will experience.

3- Get Physically Ready

Find a comfortable place where you feel relaxed and at ease. Ideally, you should sit up straight, with both feet flat on the floor. Hold the string or chain of your pendulum between your thumb and forefinger of the hand that you write with. There should be at least 2 or 3 inches between your fingers and the pendulum. Be sure that your arm and elbow are not resting on anything.

4- Focus Your Energy

All your attention and energy should be focused on your

pendulum. Any pendulum chart that you are using should be observed through your peripheral vision as you hold your full attention on your pendulum.

5- Set Your Intention

Be very clear on what outcome you hope to achieve by using your intention. You also want to make it clear that your intention is to only receive guidance that is for your highest and best good.

An example would be to hold your pendulum as you say:
My intention with this exercise is to receive truthful answers which will serve the positive and higher purpose of everyone involved.

6- Connecting with Your Subconscious Mind

Using a pendulum all starts with a strong and positive connection with your subconscious mind.

To do this, take a deep breath and allow yourself to relax. Ask your pendulum to move in some way as an indication you are connected to your subconscious mind.

7- Program Your Pendulum for Your Subconscious Mind

Once a connection with your subconscious mind has been established, you need to program your pendulum to communicate with your subconscious mind.

Follow these steps to program your pendulum for communication with your subconscious mind:

- Hold your pendulum so that it is hanging about two inches above the direct center of your **Yes or No Pendulum Chart.**

- To train your Pendulum and your subconscious mind to both understand the direction that represents Yes, swing the pendulum forwards and back as you repeat the following statement three times:

The Pendulum

> *This is the direction to represent **Yes** with my subconscious mind. (3 times)*

- To train your Pendulum and your subconscious mind to both understand the direction that represents No, swing the pendulum from left to right as you repeat three times:

*This is the direction to represent **No** with my subconscious mind. (3 times)*

- To train your Pendulum and your subconscious mind to both understand the direction that represents Maybe, swing the pendulum on an angle from top right to bottom left as you repeat three times:

*This is the direction to represent **Maybe** with my subconscious mind. (3 times)*

- To train your Pendulum and your subconscious mind to both understand the direction that represents Rephrase Question, swing the Pendulum on an angle from top left to bottom right as you repeat three times:

*This is the direction to represent **Rephrase Question** with my subconscious mind. (3 times)*

8- Test the Programing

At this point you want to test that your subconscious mind has accepted the directions you have just programmed using your pendulum. This testing will be a two-step process.

The first step in testing your pendulum is to focus all your attention on the pendulum as you repeat the following statements one at a time:

- *Show me the direction that represents **yes**.*
  Stay focused on this statement until your pendulum moves in the direction that represents yes. If your pendulum should move in any other direction, then you must take the time to go back and program your pendulum again.

- *Show me the direction that represents **no**.*

Stay focused on this statement until your pendulum moves in the direction that represents no. If your pendulum should move in any other direction, then you must take the time to go back and program your pendulum again.

- *Show me the direction that represents **maybe**.*
  Stay focused on this statement until your pendulum moves in the direction that represents maybe. If your pendulum should move in any other direction, then you must take the time to go back and program your pendulum again.

- *Show me the direction that represents **not sure**.*
  Stay focused on this statement until your pendulum moves in the direction that represents not sure. If your pendulum should move in any other direction, then you must take the time to go back and program your pendulum again.

In the second step to testing your pendulum, you will ask your pendulum a series of **yes** or **no** questions that you already know the answers to.

Examples of possible testing questions may include:

- *Is my name _____?*
- *Is my address _____?*
- *Is my age _____?*

Your objective with this test is to make sure that **yes** is yes, and **no** is no.

If the signals are not coming out right, go back and repeat the programing of yes and no until the test works out positively.

9- Subconscious Commitment

You want a commitment from your subconscious mind that it is willing to work with you to achieve the best possible results with your pendulum.

To establish a subconscious commitment, ask your pendulum the following questions:

- *My intention with using this pendulum is to help myself in a positive and healthy way. Does my subconscious mind understand my positive intention?*

- *To achieve the best possible results with the pendulum I need the full cooperation of my subconscious mind. Is my subconscious mind willing to work with me to achieve the best possible results?*

Only continue if your subconscious mind responds yes to each of these questions.

10- Program Your Pendulum for Scale or Range

Now you can program your pendulum to recognize the **scale** you are using. Using the Scale or Range Pendulum Chart at the back of the book will help with focus.

- Hold your pendulum directly above the black dot at the base of the Scale or Range Chart. This dot will always be your Starting Point when using a Scale or Range Chart..

- To train your Pendulum and your subconscious mind to both understand the direction that represents **"Low"** on the scale, swing the pendulum forwards and back in the direction of **"0"** on your Scale or Range Pendulum Chart as you repeat the following statement three times:

*This is the direction to represent **"0"** (or Low) with my subconscious mind. (3 times)*

- Stop your pendulum and again hold it directly above black dot that represents the **starting point.**

- To train your Pendulum and your subconscious mind to both understand the direction that represents **"High"**, swing pendulum forwards and back in the direction of **"100"** on your Scale or Range Pendulum Chart as you repeat the following statement three times:

*This is the direction to represent **"100"** (or High) with my subconscious mind. (3 times)*

11- Test the Programing

Now it is time to test that your subconscious mind has accepted the programming for the **scale** you have chosen to work with. To test this, you simply need to ask your pendulum to show you specific directions.

Examples of possible testing questions may include:

- Show me the direction for _____ (one end of the scale).
- Show me the direction for _____ (the other end of the scale).

Your objective with this test is to make sure that your subconscious mind has accepted the **scale** as you have defined it.

If the signals are not correct, go back repeat the programing of a **scale** until the test works out positively.

12- Using your Pendulum with a Scale

The **scale** is based on a range and your pendulum will help you adjust your energy so that you can move along the **scale** to a point that is most desirable to you.

Some possible **scale ranges** include:
- Low to High
- Negative to Positive
- Relaxed to Stressed
- Victim to Empowered
- Procrastinate to Action
- Scarcity to Abundance

Anything where there are two opposites can be used as the ends of the **scale**.

Where am I on the Scale

Once the end points of the scale have been programmed, the first question to ask is: *Where am I now on this scale?*

Once you are clear on where you are on the **scale** you can focus your thoughts on moving in the desired direction and allow the pendulum to adjust to reflect the changes in your inner focus.

Scale Example

Using a desire to increase your positive energy as an example, you would focus your thoughts by repeating, over and over:

With every breath I take I allow my positive energy to increase more and more.

As you repeat this statement over and over, notice how your pendulum starts to move, much like a meter, in the direction of higher positive energy, as your energy level increases.

If the answer is **not clear,** ask your pendulum to show you a more clear and easier to see answer.

13- Clear the Pendulum

After you have completed your pendulum exercise, it is important that you **clear your pendulum** so that it is certain that you are finished with that exercise and you are ready to move on to the next exercise.

To clear your pendulum, simply hold the weight of your pendulum in the palm of your other hand. This will relax the energy in your pendulum and allow it to prepare for the next question.

14- Say Thank You to Your Pendulum

While you are holding the weight of your Pendulum in your hands, say *thank you to your Pendulum for allowing you to experience all the benefits of the exercise.* .

15- Saying Thank You to Your Subconscious Mind

It is important to say *thank you* to your subconscious mind for allowing you to experience all the benefits of this exercise.

16- Back to Full Awareness

After you say thank you to your subconscious mind, you can take a deep breath and bring yourself back to full awareness.

The Pendulum

Specific Uses For Your Pendulum

What the Pendulum Can be Used For

In this section we will look at how to use your pendulum skills to improve specific areas of your life.

We will look at exercises for:
Nutritional Deficiencies
Increase Your Energy Level
Relax
Healing Energy to a Specific Body Part
Vibrational Alignment with Money
Letting Go of a Negative Emotion
Improve the Law of Attraction
Connecting with Spirit Guides

Using Your Pendulum To Identify Nutritional Deficiencies

Identify Nutritional Deficiencies

When you use your Pendulum to connect with your Subconscious Mind, it is possible to ask your Subconscious Mind questions to identify any nutritional deficiencies.

Questions that you may want to ask during the exercise include:
Do I need more vitamin ____ in my diet?
Do I need less vitamin ____ in my diet?
Do I need to drink more water?

The following steps will help you to work with your Pendulum and your Subconscious mind in order to identify Nutritional Deficiencies:

The **Yes or No Pendulum Chart** at the back of this book will help with Yes or No answers.

1- Get Emotionally Ready

Your pendulum will take on your emotional energy, so it is very important that you are in a positive emotional state and feeling relaxed whenever you use your pendulum.

Breathe easy and allow yourself to relax before you begin using your pendulum.

2- Get Mentally Ready

Take a deep breath and allow yourself to relax. Clear your mind of all chatter and focus all your attention on the Pendulum exercise you are about to work through. The more mentally relaxed you feel while using your Pendulum, the stronger the results you will experience.

3- Get Physically Ready

Find a comfortable place where you feel relaxed and at ease. Ideally, you should sit up straight, with both feet flat on the floor.

Hold the string or chain of your pendulum between your thumb and forefinger of the hand that you write with. There should be at least 2 or 3 inches between your fingers and the pendulum. Be sure that your arm and elbow are not resting on anything.

4- Focus Your Energy

All your attention and energy should be focused on your pendulum. Any pendulum chart that you are using should be observed through your peripheral vision as you hold your full attention on your pendulum.

5- Set Your Intention

Be very clear on what outcome you hope to achieve by using your Pendulum. You also want to make it clear that your intention is to only receive guidance that is for your highest and best good.

An example would be to hold your pendulum as you say: ***My intention with this exercise is to receive truthful answers which will serve the positive and higher purpose of everyone involved.***

6- Connecting with Your Subconscious Mind

Using a pendulum all starts with a strong and positive connection with your subconscious mind.

To do this, take a deep breath and allow yourself to relax. Ask your pendulum to move side to side as an indication that you are connected to your subconscious mind.

7- Program Your Pendulum for the Subconscious Mind

Once your pendulum starts to move, and a connection with your subconscious mind has been established, you need to program your pendulum to communicate with your subconscious mind.

Follow these steps to program your pendulum for communication with your subconscious mind:

- Hold your pendulum so that it is hanging about two inches above the direct center of your **Yes or No Pendulum Chart**.

- To train your Pendulum and your subconscious mind to both understand the direction that represents Yes, swing the pendulum forwards and back as you repeat the following statement three times:
  *This is the direction to represent **Yes** with my subconscious mind. (3 times)*

- To train your Pendulum and your subconscious mind to both understand the direction that represents No, swing the pendulum from left to right as you repeat three times:
  *This is the direction to represent **No** with my subconscious mind. (3 times)*

- To train your Pendulum and your subconscious mind to both understand the direction that represents Maybe, swing the pendulum on an angle from top right to bottom left as you repeat three times:
  *This is the direction to represent **Maybe** with my subconscious mind. (3 times)*

- To train your Pendulum and your subconscious mind to both understand the direction that represents Rephrase Question, swing the Pendulum on an angle from top left to bottom right as you repeat three times:

*This is the direction to represent **Rephrase Question** with my subconscious mind. (3 times)*

8- Test the Programing

At this point you want to test that your subconscious mind has accepted the directions you have just programmed using your Pendulum. This testing will be a two-step process.

The first step in testing your pendulum is to focus all your attention on the pendulum as you repeat the following statements one at a time:

- *Show me the direction that represents **yes**.*
  Stay focused on this statement until your pendulum moves in the direction that represents Yes. If your pendulum should move in any other direction, then you must take the time to go back and program your pendulum again.

- *Show me the direction that represents **No**.*
  Stay focused on this statement until your pendulum moves in the direction that represents No. If your pendulum should move in any other direction, then you must take the time to go back and program your pendulum again.

- *Show me the direction that represents **Maybe**.*
  Stay focused on this statement until your pendulum moves in the direction that represents maybe. If your pendulum should move in any other direction, then you must take the time to go back and program your pendulum again.

- *Show me the direction that represents **Rephrase Question**.*
  Stay focused on this statement until your pendulum moves in the direction that represents Rephrase Question. If your pendulum should move in any other direction, then you must take the time to go back and program your pendulum again.

In the second step to test the programming of your pendulum, you will ask your pendulum a series of **Yes or No** questions that you already know the answers to.

Examples of possible testing questions may include:

- *Is my name _____?*
- *Is my address _____?*
- *Is my age _____?*

Your objective with this test is to make sure that "**Yes**" **is yes**, and "**No**" **is no**.

If any of the answers you receive are incorrect, go back and repeat the programing of Yes and No until the test works out positively.

9- Subconscious Commitment

You want a commitment from your subconscious mind that it is willing to work with you to achieve the best possible results with your pendulum.

To establish a subconscious commitment, ask your pendulum the following questions:

- *My intention with using this pendulum is to help myself in a positive and healthy way. Does my subconscious mind understand my positive intention?*

- *To achieve the best possible results with the pendulum I need the full cooperation of my subconscious mind. Is my subconscious mind willing to work with me to achieve the best possible results?*

Only continue if your subconscious mind responds "Yes" to each of these questions. If you receive a "No" answer, you should take a break and return some other time to work with your pendulum.

10- Ask Specific Questions Related to Nutritional Deficiencies

Questions should be clear and understandable and should always lead to a Yes or No answer. Questions should only be about you.

Be sure that your Pendulum comes to a complete stop between each question so that nothing can influence the answer to the next question.

Questions that you may want to ask during the exercise include:
Do I need more vitamin _____ in my diet?
Do I need less vitamin _____ in my diet?
Do I need to drink more water?

If the Pendulum is not moving enough to receive a clear answer, ask your pendulum to show you a clearer and easier to see answer.

11- Clear the Pendulum

After you have received an answer to your specific question it is important that you **clear your pendulum** so that it is clear that you are finished with that question and you are ready to move on to the next question. To clear your pendulum, simply hold the weight of your pendulum in the palm of your other hand. This will relax the energy in your pendulum and allow it to prepare for the next question.

12- Say Thank You to Your Pendulum

While you are holding the weight of your Pendulum in your hands, say *thank you to your Pendulum for allowing you to experience all the benefits of the exercise.* .

13- Saying Thank You to Subconscious Mind

It is important to say thank you after you receive an answer to each of your questions. This will keep you in a positive frame of mind where the focus is gratitude. It is also important to say thank you for all the guidance you have received when you have finished asking all your questions and you are about to end the session with your pendulum.

14- Back to Full Awareness

After you say thank you to your subconscious mind, you can take a deep breath and bring yourself back to full awareness.

Using Your Pendulum to Increase Your Energy Level

Adjust Your Energy Level

In this exercise, we will use the Low – High Range Pendulum Chart to help with our focus.

1- Get Emotionally Ready

Your pendulum will take on your emotional energy, so it is very important that you are in a positive and relaxed emotional state whenever you use your pendulum.

Breathe easy and allow yourself to relax before you begin using your pendulum.

2- Get Mentally Ready

Take a deep breath and allow yourself to relax. Clear your mind of all chatter and focus all your attention on the Pendulum exercise you are about to work through. The more mentally relaxed you feel while using your Pendulum, the stronger the results you will experience.

3- Get Physically Ready

Find a comfortable place where you feel relaxed and at ease. Ideally, you should sit up straight, with both feet flat on the floor. Hold the string or chain of your pendulum between your thumb and forefinger of the hand that you write with. There should be at least 2 or 3 inches between your fingers and the pendulum. Be sure that your arm and elbow are not resting on anything.

4- Focus Your Energy

All your attention and energy should be focused on your pendulum. Any pendulum chart that you are using should be observed through your peripheral vision as you hold your full attention on your pendulum.

5- Set Your Intention

Be sure to focus all your attention on your desire to use the Pendulum as a tool to help you Increase Your Energy Level.

An example would be to hold your pendulum as you say:

My intention with this exercise is to increase my energy level in a healthy and safe way.

6- Connecting with Your Subconscious Mind

Using a pendulum all starts with a strong and positive connection with your subconscious mind.

To do this, take a deep breath and allow yourself to relax. Ask your pendulum to move in some way as an indication you are connected to your subconscious mind.

- **Program Your Pendulum for Your Subconscious Mind**

    Once a connection with your subconscious mind has been established, you need to program your pendulum to communicate with your subconscious mind.

    Follow these steps to program your pendulum for communication with your subconscious mind:
    - Hold your pendulum so that it is hanging about two inches above the direct center of your **Yes or No Pendulum Chart**.

- To train your Pendulum and your subconscious mind to both understand the direction that represents Yes, swing the pendulum forwards and back as you repeat the following statement three times:

*This is the direction to represent **Yes** with my subconscious mind. (3 times)*

- To train your Pendulum and your subconscious mind to both understand the direction that represents No, swing the pendulum from left to right as you repeat three times:

*This is the direction to represent **No** with my subconscious mind. (3 times)*

- To train your Pendulum and your subconscious mind to both understand the direction that represents Maybe, swing the pendulum on an angle from top right to bottom left as you repeat three times:

*This is the direction to represent **Maybe** with my subconscious mind. (3 times)*

- To train your Pendulum and your subconscious mind to both understand the direction that represents Rephrase Question, swing the Pendulum on an angle from top left to bottom right as you repeat three times:

This is the direction to represent **Rephrase Question** *with my subconscious mind. (3 times)*

8- Test the Programing

At this point you want to test that your subconscious mind has accepted the directions you have just programmed using your pendulum. This testing will be a two-step process.

The first step in testing your pendulum is to focus all your attention on the pendulum as you repeat the following statements one at a time:

- *Show me the direction that represents* ***yes***.

Stay focused on this statement until your pendulum moves in the direction that represents yes. If your pendulum should move in any other direction, then you must take the time to go back and program your pendulum again.

- *Show me the direction that represents **no**.*
  Stay focused on this statement until your pendulum moves in the direction that represents no. If your pendulum should move in any other direction, then you must take the time to go back and program your pendulum again.

- *Show me the direction that represents **maybe**.*
  Stay focused on this statement until your pendulum moves in the direction that represents maybe. If your pendulum should move in any other direction, then you must take the time to go back and program your pendulum again.

- *Show me the direction that represents **not sure**.*
  Stay focused on this statement until your pendulum moves in the direction that represents not sure. If your pendulum should move in any other direction, then you must take the time to go back and program your pendulum again.

In the second step to testing your pendulum, you will ask your pendulum a series of **yes** or **no** questions that you already know the answers to.

Examples of possible testing questions may include:

- *Is my name _____?*
- *Is my address _____?*
- *Is my age _____?*

Your objective with this test is to make sure that **yes** is yes, and **no** is no.

If the signals are not coming out right, go back and repeat the programing of yes and no until the test works out positively.

9- Subconscious Commitment

You want a commitment from your subconscious mind that it is willing to work with you to achieve the best possible results with your pendulum.

To establish a subconscious commitment, ask your pendulum the following questions:

- *My intention with using this pendulum is to help myself in a positive and healthy way. Does my subconscious mind understand my positive intention?*

- *To achieve the best possible results with the pendulum I need the full cooperation of my subconscious mind. Is my subconscious mind willing to work with me to achieve the best possible results?*

Only continue if your subconscious mind responds yes to each of these questions.

10- Program Your Pendulum for Scale or Range

Now you can program your pendulum to recognize the **scale** you are using. Using the Scale or Range Pendulum Chart at the back of the book will help with focus.

- Hold your pendulum directly above the black dot at the base of the Scale or Range Chart. This dot will always be your Starting Point when using a Scale or Range Chart..

- To train your Pendulum and your subconscious mind to both understand the direction that represents **"Low"** on the scale, swing the pendulum forwards and back in the direction of **"0"** on your Scale or Range Pendulum Chart as you repeat the following statement three times:
This is the direction to represent "0" (or Low) with my subconscious mind. (3 times)

- Stop your pendulum and again hold it directly above black dot that represents the **starting point.**

  - To train your Pendulum and your subconscious mind to both understand the direction that represents **"High"**, swing pendulum forwards and back in the direction of **"100"** on your Scale or Range Pendulum Chart as you repeat the following statement three times:

*This is the direction to represent **"100"** (or High) with my subconscious mind. (3 times)*

11- Test the Programing

Now it is time to test that your subconscious mind has accepted the programing for the **scale** you have chosen to work with. To test this, you simply need to ask your pendulum to show you specific directions.

Examples of possible testing questions may include:

- Show me the direction for _____ (one end of the scale).
- Show me the direction for _____ (the other end of the scale).

Your objective with this test is to make sure that your subconscious mind has accepted the **scale** as you have defined it.

If the signals are not correct, go back repeat the programing of a **scale** until the test works out positively.

12- Using your Pendulum to Increase Energy

Now that you have clearly defined the range for your scale, you are ready to use your Pendulum to increase your Energy Level.

13- Where am I on the Scale

Ask your Pendulum to use the scale to show you where your energy level is right now.

14- Increase Your Energy Level

As the pendulum swings to indicate your current energy level, direct your Subconscious Mind to increase your energy level by repeating the following statement over and over.

With every breath I take I allow my positive energy to increase more and more.

As you repeat this statement over and over, notice how your pendulum starts to move, much like a meter, in the direction of higher positive energy, as your energy level increases.

If the answer is **not clear,** ask your pendulum to show you a more clear and easier to see answer.

15- Clear the Pendulum

After you have completed your pendulum exercise, it is important that you **clear your pendulum** so that it is certain that you are finished with that exercise and you are ready to move on to the next exercise.

To clear your pendulum, simply hold the weight of your pendulum in the palm of your other hand. This will relax the energy in your pendulum and allow it to prepare for the next question.

16- Say Thank You to Your Pendulum

While you are holding the weight of your Pendulum in your hands, say *thank you to your Pendulum for allowing you to experience all the benefits of the exercise.*
.

17- Saying Thank You to Your Subconscious Mind

It is important to say *thank you* to your subconscious mind for allowing you to experience all the benefits of this exercise.

18- Back to Full Awareness

After you say thank you to your subconscious mind, you can take a deep breath and bring yourself back to full awareness.

Using Your Pendulum to Relax

Relax

In this exercise we will again use the Pendulum Chart for Scale or Range. A specific Pendulum Chart has been provided for the range from Relaxed to Stressed.

Work through each of the following steps to allow yourself to benefit from using your Pendulum to Relax.

1- Get Emotionally Ready

Your pendulum will take on your emotional energy, so it is very important that you are in a positive and relaxed emotional state whenever you use your pendulum.

Breathe easy and allow yourself to relax before you begin using your pendulum.

2- Get Mentally Ready

Take a deep breath and allow

yourself to relax. Clear your mind of all chatter and focus all your attention on the Pendulum exercise you are about to work through. The more mentally relaxed you feel while using your Pendulum, the stronger the results you will experience.

3- Get Physically Ready

Find a comfortable place where you feel relaxed and at ease. Ideally, you should sit up straight, with both feet flat on the floor. Hold the string or chain of your pendulum between your thumb and forefinger of the hand that you write with. There should be at least 2 or 3 inches between your fingers and the pendulum. Be sure that your arm and elbow are not resting on anything.

4- Focus Your Energy

All your attention and energy should be focused on your pendulum. Any pendulum chart that you are using should be observed through your peripheral vision as you hold your full attention on your pendulum.

5- Set Your Intention

Be sure to focus all your attention on your desire to use the Pendulum as a tool to help you Relax.

In order for you to feel more relaxed, you can set your intention by holding your Pendulum in both hands as you say:

My intention with this exercise is to allow myself to Relax, totally and completely, in a healthy and safe way.

6- Connecting with Your Subconscious Mind

Using a pendulum all starts with a strong and positive connection with your subconscious mind.

To do this, take a deep breath and allow yourself to relax. Ask your pendulum to move in some way as an indication you are connected to your subconscious mind.

- **Program Your Pendulum for Your Subconscious Mind**

Once a connection with your subconscious mind has been established, you need to program your pendulum to communicate with your subconscious mind.

Follow these steps to program your pendulum for communication with your subconscious mind:
- Hold your pendulum so that it is hanging about two inches above the direct center of your **Yes or No Pendulum Chart.**

- To train your Pendulum and your subconscious mind to both understand the direction that represents Yes, swing the pendulum forwards and back as you repeat the following statement three times:

*This is the direction to represent **Yes** with my subconscious mind. (3 times)*

- To train your Pendulum and your subconscious mind to both understand the direction that represents No, swing the pendulum from left to right as you repeat three times:

*This is the direction to represent **No** with my subconscious mind. (3 times)*

- To train your Pendulum and your subconscious mind to both understand the direction that represents Maybe, swing the pendulum on an angle from top right to bottom left as you repeat three times:

*This is the direction to represent **Maybe** with my subconscious mind. (3 times)*

- To train your Pendulum and your subconscious mind to both understand the direction that represents Rephrase Question, swing the Pendulum on an angle from top left to bottom right as you repeat three times:

*This is the direction to represent **Rephrase Question** with my subconscious mind. (3 times)*

8- Test the Programing

At this point you want to test that your subconscious mind has accepted the directions you have just programmed using your pendulum. This testing will be a two-step process.

The first step in testing your pendulum is to focus all your attention on the pendulum as you repeat the following statements one at a time:

- *Show me the direction that represents **yes**.*

Stay focused on this statement until your pendulum moves in the direction that represents yes. If your pendulum should move in any other direction, then you must take the time to go back and program your pendulum again.

- *Show me the direction that represents **no**.*

Stay focused on this statement until your pendulum moves in the direction that represents no. If your pendulum should move in any other direction, then you must take the time to go back and program your pendulum again.

- *Show me the direction that represents **maybe**.*

Stay focused on this statement until your pendulum moves in the direction that represents maybe. If your pendulum should move in any other direction, then you must take the time to go back and program your pendulum again.

- *Show me the direction that represents **not sure**.*

Stay focused on this statement until your pendulum moves in the direction that represents not sure. If your pendulum should move in any other direction, then you must take the time to go back and program your pendulum again.

In the second step to testing your pendulum, you will ask your pendulum a series of **yes** or **no** questions that you already know the answers to.

Examples of possible testing questions may include:

- *Is my name _____?*
- *Is my address _____?*
- *Is my age _____?*

Your objective with this test is to make sure that **yes** is yes, and **no** is no.

If the signals are not coming out right, go back and repeat the programing of yes and no until the test works out positively.

9- Subconscious Commitment

You want a commitment from your subconscious mind that it is willing to work with you to achieve the best possible results with your pendulum.

To establish a subconscious commitment, ask your pendulum the following questions:

- *My intention with using this pendulum is to help myself in a positive and healthy way. Does my subconscious mind understand my positive intention?*

- *To achieve the best possible results with the pendulum I need the full cooperation of my subconscious mind. Is my subconscious mind willing to work with me to achieve the best possible results?*

Only continue if your subconscious mind responds yes to each of these questions.

10- Program Your Pendulum for Scale or Range

Now you can program your pendulum to recognize the **scale** you are using. Using the Scale or Range Pendulum Chart at the back of the book will help with focus.

- Hold your pendulum directly above the black dot at the base of the Scale or Range Chart. This dot will always be your Starting Point when using a Scale or Range Chart..

- To train your Pendulum and your subconscious mind to both understand the direction that represents **"Low"** on the scale, swing the pendulum forwards and back in the direction of **"0"** on your Scale or Range Pendulum Chart as you repeat the following statement three times:

*This is the direction to represent **"0"** (or Low) with my subconscious mind. (3 times)*

- Stop your pendulum and again hold it directly above black dot that represents the **starting point.**

- To train your Pendulum and your subconscious mind to both understand the direction that represents **"High"**, swing pendulum forwards and back in the direction of **"100"** on your Scale or Range Pendulum Chart as you repeat the following statement three times:

*This is the direction to represent **"100"** (or High) with my subconscious mind. (3 times)*

11- Test the Programing

Now it is time to test that your subconscious mind has accepted the programing for the **scale** you have chosen to work with. To test this, you simply need to ask your pendulum to show you specific directions.

Examples of possible testing questions may include:
- Show me the direction for _____ (one end of the scale).
- Show me the direction for _____ (the other end of the scale).

Your objective with this test is to make sure that your subconscious mind has accepted the **scale** as you have defined it.

If the signals are not correct, go back repeat the programing of a **scale** until the test works out positively.

12- Using your Pendulum to Relax

Now that you have clearly defined the range for your scale, you are ready to use your Pendulum to Relax.

In this exercise, we will guide the Pendulum to move from right to left, as an indication we are feeling more and more relaxed.

13- Where am I on the Scale

Ask your Pendulum to use the scale to show you where your energy level is right now.

14- Allow Yourself to Relax

As the pendulum swings to indicate your current level of relaxation, direct your Subconscious Mind to allow you to relax more and by repeating the following statement over and over.

With every breath I take I allow myself to feel more and more relaxed.

As you repeat this statement over and over, notice how your pendulum starts to move, much like a
meter, in the direction of greater relaxation.

If the answer is **not clear,** ask your pendulum to show you a more clear and easier to see answer.

15- Clear the Pendulum

After you have completed your pendulum exercise, it is important that you **clear your pendulum** so that it is certain that you are finished with that exercise and you are ready to move on to the next exercise.

To clear your pendulum, simply hold the weight of your pendulum in the palm of your other hand. This will relax the energy in your pendulum and allow it to prepare for the next question.

16- Say Thank You to Your Pendulum

While you are holding the weight of your Pendulum in your hands, say *thank you to your Pendulum for allowing you to experience all the benefits of the exercise.* .

17- Saying Thank You to Your Subconscious Mind

It is important to say *thank you* to your subconscious mind for allowing you to experience all the benefits of this exercise.

18- Back to Full Awareness

After you say thank you to your subconscious mind, you can take a deep breath and bring yourself back to full awareness.

Using Your Pendulum to Send Healing Energy to a Specific Body Part

Send Healing Energy to a Specific Body Part

In this exercise, we will start by using our **Yes – No** Pendulum Chart to create a connection with our Subconscious Mind, then we will use our **Yes – No** Pendulum Chart to create a second connection with the specific body part, and finally we will use the **Low – High** Range Pendulum Chart to allow us to provide Healing Energy to the specific Body Part.

1- Get Emotionally Ready

Take several slow deep breaths and allow yourself to relax before you begin the exercise.

2- Get Mentally Ready

Take a deep breath and allow yourself to relax. Clear your mind of all chatter and focus all your attention on the Pendulum exercise you are about to work through. The more mentally relaxed you feel while using your Pendulum, the stronger the results you will experience.

3- Get Physically Ready

Find a comfortable place where you feel relaxed and at ease. Ideally, you should sit up straight, with both feet flat on the floor. Hold the string or chain of your pendulum between your thumb and forefinger of the hand that you write with. There should be at least 2 or 3 inches between your fingers and the pendulum. Be sure that your arm and elbow are not resting on anything.

4- Set Your Intention

In order for you to send healing energy to a specific body part, you can set your intention by holding your Pendulum in both hands as you say:

My intention with this exercise is to direct Healing Energy to my ___ in a healthy and safe way.

5- Focus Your Energy

Now allow your Pendulum to hang free. It should be still as you allow it to hang there.

Focus your attention on your Pendulum. Stare at your Pendulum. Place all your concentration on your pendulum.

Allow yourself to be aware of your Pendulum Chart through your peripheral vision as you hold your full attention on your Pendulum.

6- Connecting with Your Subconscious Mind

Take a deep breath and allow yourself to relax. Ask your Pendulum to move in some way as an indication you are connected to your subconscious mind. Be patient and wait for your Pendulum to move as the sign you are connected to your subconscious mind.

7- Program Your Pendulum for Your Subconscious Mind

- Hold your pendulum so that it is hanging about two inches above the direct center of your **Yes or No Pendulum Chart.**

- Swing the pendulum forwards and back as you repeat the following statement three times:

*This is the direction to represent **Yes** with my subconscious mind. (3 times)*

- Swing the pendulum from left to right as you repeat three times:

*This is the direction to represent **No** with my subconscious mind. (3 times)*

- Swing the pendulum on an angle from top right to bottom left as you repeat three times:

*This is the direction to represent **Maybe** with my subconscious mind. (3 times)*

- Swing the Pendulum on an angle from top left to bottom right as you repeat three times:

*This is the direction to represent **Rephrase Question** with my subconscious mind. (3 times)*

8- Test the Programing

Test 1:

Focus all your attention on the pendulum as you repeat the following statements one at a time:

- *Show me the direction that represents **yes**.*
  Stay focused on this statement until your pendulum moves in the direction that represents yes. If your pendulum should move in any other direction, then you must take the time to go back and program your pendulum again.

- *Show me the direction that represents **no**.*

Stay focused on this statement until your pendulum moves in the direction that represents no. If your pendulum should move in any other direction, then you must take the time to go back and program your pendulum again.

- *Show me the direction that represents **maybe**.*

Stay focused on this statement until your pendulum moves in the direction that represents maybe. If your pendulum should move in any other direction, then you must take the time to go back and program your pendulum again.

- *Show me the direction that represents **not sure**.*

Stay focused on this statement until your pendulum moves in the direction that represents not sure. If your pendulum should move in any other direction, then you must take the time to go back and program your pendulum again.

Test 2:

Ask two or three questions where your Pendulum will answer either Yes or No. Be sure you know the answer with certainty.

Examples of possible testing questions may include:

- *Is my name _____?*
- *Is my address _____?*
- *Is my age _____?*

If the answers are not correct, go back and repeat the programing of yes and no until the test works out positively.

9- Subconscious Commitment

To establish a subconscious commitment, ask your pendulum the following questions:

- *My intention with using this pendulum is to help myself in a positive and healthy way. Does my subconscious mind understand my positive intention?*

- *To achieve the best possible results with the pendulum I need the full cooperation of my subconscious mind. Is my subconscious mind willing to work with me to achieve the best possible results?*

- *In this exercise I want to send Healing to my _____ (specific body part) in a healthy and safe way. Is my subconscious mind willing to send this Healing Energy in a healthy and safe way?*

Only continue if your subconscious mind responds yes to each of these questions.

10- Program Your Pendulum for Scale or Range

Using the Scale or Range Pendulum Chart at the back of the book will help with focus.

- Swing the pendulum forwards and back in the direction of **"0"** on your Scale or Range Pendulum Chart as you repeat:

This is the direction to represent "0" (or Low) with my subconscious mind. (3 times)

- Stop your pendulum and again hold it directly above black dot that represents the **starting point.**

- This time swing the pendulum forwards and back in the direction of **"100"** on your Scale or Range Pendulum Chart as you repeat:

This is the direction to represent "100" (or High) with my subconscious mind. (3 times)

11- Test the Programing

Now ask your pendulum to show you specific directions as a test.

- Show me the direction for Low.
- Show me the direction for High.

If the signals are not correct, go back repeat the programing of a **scale** until the test works out positively.

12- Connect with Specific Body Part

Take a deep breath and allow yourself to relax even more. Ask your Pendulum to move in some way as an indication you are connected to the specific body part. Be patient and wait for your Pendulum to move as the sign you are connected to your specific body part.

13- Send Healing Energy to Specific Body Part

Hold your Pendulum over the Black Dot and direct it to send Healing Energy to the specific body part. Tell you Pendulum that you want it to move as an indication of the level of Healing Energy that is being sent.

Direct your Subconscious Mind to increase the Healing Energy as you repeat the following statement over and over.

With every breath I take I allow Healing Energy to go to ___ in a positive and healthy way.

If the answer is **not clear,** ask your pendulum to show you a more clear and easier to see answer.

14- Clear the Pendulum

After you feel that you have sent enough Healing Energy for this session, it is time to **clear your pendulum.**

Hold the weight of your pendulum in the palm of your other hand. This will relax the energy in your pendulum and allow it to prepare for the next question.

15- Say Thank You to Your Pendulum

While you are holding the weight of your Pendulum in your hands, say *thank you to your Pendulum for allowing you to experience all the benefits of the exercise.* .

16- Say Thank You to Your Subconscious Mind

While continuing to hold the weight of your Pendulum in your hands, say *thank you* to your subconscious mind for allowing you to experience all the benefits of this exercise.

17- Back to Full Awareness

After you say thank you to your subconscious mind, you can take a deep breath and bring yourself back to full awareness.

Using Your Pendulum To Create a Vibrational Alignment with Money

Vibrational Alignment with Money

In this exercise, we will start by using our ***Yes – No*** Pendulum Chart to create a connection with our Subconscious Mind, and then we will use the ***Low – High*** Range Pendulum Chart to increase our vibrational energy with money.

1- Get Emotionally Ready

Take several slow deep breaths and allow yourself to relax before you begin the exercise.

2- Get Mentally Ready

Take a deep breath and allow yourself to relax. Clear your mind of all chatter and focus all your attention on the Pendulum exercise you are about to work through. The more mentally relaxed you feel while using your Pendulum, the stronger the results you will experience.

3- Get Physically Ready

Find a comfortable place where you feel relaxed and at ease. Ideally, you should

sit up straight, with both feet flat on the floor. Hold the string or chain of your pendulum between your thumb and forefinger of the hand that you write with. There should be at least 2 or 3 inches between your fingers and the pendulum. Be sure that your arm and elbow are not resting on anything.

4- Set Your Intention

In order for you to create a vibrational alignment with money, you must first set your intention by holding your Pendulum in both hands as you say:

My intention with this exercise is to create a vibrational alignment with money.

5- Focus Your Energy

Now allow your Pendulum to hang free. It should be still as you allow it to hang there.

Focus your attention on your Pendulum. Stare at your Pendulum. Place all your concentration on your pendulum.

Allow yourself to be aware of your Pendulum Chart through your peripheral vision as you hold your full attention on your Pendulum.

6- Connecting with Your Subconscious Mind

Take a deep breath and allow yourself to relax. Ask your Pendulum to move in some way as an indication you are connected to your subconscious mind. Be patient and wait for your Pendulum to move as the sign you are connected to your subconscious mind.

7- Program Your Pendulum for Your Subconscious Mind

- Hold your pendulum so that it is hanging about two inches above the direct center of your **Yes or No Pendulum Chart.**

- Swing the pendulum forwards and back as you repeat the following statement three times:

This is the direction to represent **Yes** *with my subconscious mind. (3 times)*

- Swing the pendulum from left to right as you repeat three times:

*This is the direction to represent **No** with my subconscious mind. (3 times)*

- Swing the pendulum on an angle from top right to bottom left as you repeat three times:

*This is the direction to represent **Maybe** with my subconscious mind. (3 times)*

- Swing the Pendulum on an angle from top left to bottom right as you repeat three times:

*This is the direction to represent **Rephrase Question** with my subconscious mind. (3 times)*

8- Test the Programing

Test 1:

Focus all your attention on the pendulum as you repeat the following statements one at a time:

- *Show me the direction that represents **yes**.*

Stay focused on this statement until your pendulum moves in the direction that

represents yes. If your pendulum should move in any other direction, then you must take the time to go back and program your pendulum again.

- *Show me the direction that represents **no**.*
  Stay focused on this statement until your pendulum moves in the direction that represents no. If your pendulum should move in any other direction, then you must take the time to go back and program your pendulum again.

- *Show me the direction that represents **maybe**.*
  Stay focused on this statement until your pendulum moves in the direction that represents maybe. If your pendulum should move in any other direction, then you must take the time to go back and program your pendulum again.

- *Show me the direction that represents **not sure**.*
  Stay focused on this statement until your pendulum moves in the direction that represents not sure. If your pendulum should move in any other direction, then you must take the time to go back and program your pendulum again.

Test 2:

Ask two or three questions where your Pendulum will answer either Yes or No. Be sure you know the answer with certainty.

Examples of possible testing questions may include:

- *Is my name _____?*
- *Is my address _____?*
- *Is my age _____?*

If the answers are not correct, go back and repeat the programing of yes and no until the test works out positively.

9- Subconscious Commitment

To establish a subconscious commitment, ask your pendulum the following questions:

- *My intention with using this pendulum is to help myself in a positive and healthy way. Does my subconscious mind understand my positive intention?*

- *To achieve the best possible results with the pendulum I need the full cooperation of my subconscious mind. Is my subconscious mind willing to work with me to achieve the best possible results?*

- *In this exercise I want to create a stronger alignment with money. Is my subconscious mind willing to work with me to create this stronger alignment with money in a healthy and safe way?*

Only continue if your subconscious mind responds yes to each of these questions.

10- Program Your Pendulum for Scale or Range

Using the Scale or Range Pendulum Chart at the back of the book will help with focus.

- Swing the pendulum forwards and back in the direction of **"0"** on your Scale or Range Pendulum Chart as you repeat:

*This is the direction to represent **"0"** (or Low) with my subconscious mind. (3 times)*

Stop your pendulum and again hold it directly above black dot that represents the **starting point.**

- This time swing the pendulum forwards and back in the direction of **"100"** on your Scale or Range Pendulum Chart as you repeat:

*This is the direction to represent **"100"** (or High) with my subconscious mind. (3 times)*

11- Test the Programing

Now ask your pendulum to show you specific directions as a test.

- Show me the direction for Low.
- Show me the direction for High.

If the signals are not correct, go back repeat the programing of a **scale** until the test works out positively.

12- Increase Your alignment with Money

Hold your Pendulum over the Black Dot and direct it to increase your alignment with money. Tell your Pendulum that you want it to move as an indication of the increasing alignment with money.

Direct your Subconscious Mind to increase the alignment with money as you repeat the following statement over and over.

With every breath I take I increase my alignment with money in a positive and healthy way.

If the answer is **not clear,** ask your pendulum to show you a more clear and easier to see answer.

13- Clear the Pendulum

After you feel that you have improved your alignment with money, it is time to **clear your pendulum.**

Hold the weight of your pendulum in the palm of your other hand. This will relax the energy in your pendulum and allow it to prepare for the next question.

14- Say Thank You to Your Pendulum

While you are holding the weight of your Pendulum in your hands, say *thank you to your Pendulum for allowing you to experience all the benefits of the exercise.* .

15- Say Thank You to Your Subconscious Mind

While continuing to hold the weight of your Pendulum in your hands, say *thank you* to your subconscious mind for allowing you to experience all the benefits of this exercise.

16- Back to Full Awareness

After you say thank you to your subconscious mind, you can take a deep breath and bring yourself back to full awareness.

Using Your Pendulum to Let Go of a Negative Emotion

Letting Go of a Negative Emotion

In this exercise, we will start by using our ***Yes – No*** Pendulum Chart to create a connection with our Subconscious Mind, and then we will use the ***Low – High*** Range Pendulum Chart to let go of the negative energy associated with a specific negative emotion.

1- Get Emotionally Ready

Take several slow deep breaths and allow yourself to relax before you begin the exercise.

2- Get Mentally Ready

Take a deep breath and allow yourself to relax. Clear your mind of all chatter and focus all your attention on the Pendulum exercise you are about to work through. The more mentally relaxed you feel while using your Pendulum, the stronger the results you will experience.

3- Get Physically Ready

Find a comfortable place where you feel relaxed and at ease. Ideally, you should sit up straight, with both feet flat on the floor. Hold the string or chain of your pendulum between your thumb and forefinger of the hand that you write with. There should be at least 2 or 3 inches between your fingers and the pendulum. Be sure that your arm and elbow are not resting on anything.

4- Set Your Intention

In order for you to let go of a specific negative emotion, you must first decide on the specific negative emotion you want to clear, and then set your intention by holding your Pendulum in both hands as you say:

My intention with this exercise is to let go of ____ (a specific negative emotion) totally and completely, in a healthy and safe way.

5- Focus Your Energy

Now allow your Pendulum to hang free. It should be still as you allow it to hang there.

Focus your attention on your Pendulum. Stare at your Pendulum. Place all your concentration on your pendulum.

Allow yourself to be aware of your Pendulum Chart through your peripheral vision as you hold your full attention on your Pendulum.

6- Connecting with Your Subconscious Mind

Take a deep breath and allow yourself to relax. Ask your Pendulum to move in some way as an indication you are connected to your subconscious mind. Be patient and wait for your Pendulum to move as the sign you are connected to your subconscious mind.

- **Program Your Pendulum for Your Subconscious Mind**

- Hold your pendulum so that it is hanging about two inches above the direct center of your **Yes or No Pendulum Chart.**

- Swing the pendulum forwards and back as you repeat the following statement three times:

*This is the direction to represent **Yes** with my subconscious mind. (3 times)*

- Swing the pendulum from left to right as you repeat three times:

*This is the direction to represent **No** with my subconscious mind. (3 times)*

- Swing the pendulum on an angle from top right to bottom left as you repeat

- three times:

*This is the direction to represent **Maybe** with my subconscious mind. (3 times)*

- Swing the Pendulum on an angle from top left to bottom right as you repeat three times:

*This is the direction to represent **Rephrase Question** with my subconscious mind. (3 times)*

8- Test the Programing

Test 1:

Focus all your attention on the pendulum as you repeat the following statements one at a time:

- *Show me the direction that represents **yes**.*

Stay focused on this statement until your pendulum moves in the direction that represents yes. If your pendulum should move in any other direction, then you must take the time to go back and program your pendulum again.

- *Show me the direction that represents **no**.*

Stay focused on this statement until your pendulum moves in the direction that represents no. If your pendulum should move in any other direction, then you must take the time to go back and program your pendulum again.

- *Show me the direction that represents **maybe**.*

Stay focused on this statement until your pendulum moves in the direction that represents maybe. If your pendulum should move in any other direction, then you must take the time to go back and program your pendulum again.

- *Show me the direction that represents **not sure**.*

Stay focused on this statement until your pendulum moves in the direction that represents not sure. If your pendulum should move in any other direction, then you must take the time to go back and program your pendulum again.

Test 2:

Ask two or three questions where your Pendulum will answer either Yes or No. Be sure you know the answer with certainty.

Examples of possible testing questions may include:

- *Is my name _____?*
- *Is my address _____?*
- *Is my age _____?*

If the answers are not correct, go back and repeat the programing of yes and no until the test works out positively.

9- Subconscious Commitment

To establish a subconscious commitment, ask your pendulum the following questions:

- *My intention with using this pendulum is to help myself in a positive and healthy way. Does my subconscious mind understand my positive intention?*

- *To achieve the best possible results with the pendulum I need the full cooperation of my subconscious mind. Is my subconscious mind willing to work with me to achieve the best possible results?*

- *In this exercise I want to let go of ___ (state a specific negative emotion) totally and completely, in a healthy and safe way. Is my subconscious mind willing to work with me to let go of ___ in a healthy and safe way?*

Only continue if your subconscious mind responds yes to each of these questions.

10- Program Your Pendulum for Scale or Range

Using the Scale or Range Pendulum Chart at the back of the book will help with focus.

- Swing the pendulum forwards and back in the direction of **"0"** on your Scale or Range Pendulum Chart as you repeat:

*This is the direction to represent **"0"** (or Low) with my subconscious mind. (3 times)*

- Stop your pendulum and again hold it directly above black dot that represents the **starting point.**

- This time swing the pendulum forwards and back in the direction of **"100"** on your Scale or Range Pendulum Chart as you repeat:

*This is the direction to represent **"100"** (or High) with my subconscious mind. (3 times)*

11- Test the Programing

Now ask your pendulum to show you specific directions as a test.

- Show me the direction for Low.
- Show me the direction for High.

If the signals are not correct, go back repeat the programing of a **scale** until the test works out positively.

12- Level of Negative Emotion now

Ask your Pendulum to use the scale to show you the current level of the specific negative emotion that currently exists in your body.

13- Let Go of a Negative Emotion

As your pendulum moves to indicate your current level of that specific negative emotion, direct your subconscious mind to let go of that negative emotion.

Direct your Subconscious Mind to let go of the negative emotion as you repeat the following statement over and over.

With every breath I take my subconscious mind lets go of ___ (specific negative emotion) in a healthy and safe way.

If the answer is **not clear,** ask your pendulum to show you a more clear and easier to see answer.

Notice that the pendulum starts to move towards "0" as your subconscious mind lets go of the negative emotions.

14- Clear the Pendulum

After you feel that you have let go of the negative emotion, it is time to **clear your pendulum.**

Hold the weight of your pendulum in the palm of your other hand. This will relax the energy in your pendulum and allow it to prepare for the next question.

15- Say Thank You to Your Pendulum

While you are holding the weight of your Pendulum in your hands, say *thank you to your Pendulum for allowing you to experience all the benefits of the exercise.* .

16- Say Thank You to Your Subconscious Mind

While continuing to hold the weight of your Pendulum in your hands, say *thank you* to your subconscious mind for allowing you to experience all the benefits of this exercise.

17- Back to Full Awareness

After you say thank you to your subconscious mind, you can take a deep breath and bring yourself back to full awareness.

Using Your Pendulum to Improve the Law of Attraction

Improve the Law of Attraction

In this exercise, we will start by using our ***Yes – No*** Pendulum Chart to create a connection with our Subconscious Mind, and then we will use the ***Low – High*** Range Pendulum Chart to increase our vibrational frequency so that we are better able to benefit from the Law of Attraction.

1- Get Emotionally Ready

Take several slow deep breaths and allow yourself to relax before you begin the exercise.

2- Get Mentally Ready

Take a deep breath and allow yourself to relax. Clear your mind of all chatter and focus all your attention on the Pendulum exercise you are about to work through. The more mentally relaxed you feel while using your Pendulum, the stronger the results you will experience.

3- Get Physically Ready

Find a comfortable place where you feel relaxed and at ease. Ideally, you should sit up straight, with both feet flat on the floor. Hold the string or chain of your pendulum between your thumb and forefinger of the hand that you write with. There should be at least 2 or 3 inches between your fingers and the pendulum. Be sure that your arm and elbow are not resting on anything.

4- Set Your Intention

In order for you to increase your vibrational frequency so that you are better able to benefit from the Law of Attraction, you must set your intention by holding your Pendulum in both hands as you say:

My intention with this exercise is to increase my vibrational frequency, in a healthy and safe way, so that the Law of Attraction will work better for me. .

5- Focus Your Energy

Now allow your Pendulum to hang free. It should be still as you allow it to hang there.

Focus your attention on your Pendulum. Stare at your Pendulum. Place all your concentration on your pendulum.

Allow yourself to be aware of your Pendulum Chart through your peripheral vision as you hold your full attention on your Pendulum.

6- Connecting with Your Subconscious Mind

Take a deep breath and allow yourself to relax. Ask your Pendulum to move in some way as an indication you are connected to your subconscious mind. Be patient and wait for your Pendulum to move as the sign you are connected to your subconscious mind.

7- Program Your Pendulum for Your Subconscious Mind

- Hold your pendulum so that it is hanging about two inches above the direct center of your **Yes or No Pendulum Chart.**

- Swing the pendulum forwards and back as you repeat the following statement three times:

*This is the direction to represent **Yes** with my subconscious mind. (3 times)*

- Swing the pendulum from left to right as you repeat three times:

*This is the direction to represent **No** with my subconscious mind. (3 times)*

- Swing the pendulum on an angle from top right to bottom left as you repeat three times:

*This is the direction to represent **Maybe** with my subconscious mind. (3 times)*

- Swing the Pendulum on an angle from top left to bottom right as you repeat three times:

*This is the direction to represent **Rephrase Question** with my subconscious mind. (3 times)*

8- Test the Programing

Test 1:

Focus all your attention on the pendulum as you repeat the following statements one at a time:

- *Show me the direction that represents **yes**.*

Stay focused on this statement until your pendulum moves in the direction that represents yes. If your pendulum should move in any other direction, then you must take the time to go back and program your pendulum again.

- *Show me the direction that represents **no**.*

Stay focused on this statement until your pendulum moves in the direction that represents no. If your pendulum should move in any other direction, then you must take the time to go back and program your pendulum again.

- *Show me the direction that represents **maybe**.*

Stay focused on this statement until your pendulum moves in the direction that represents maybe. If your pendulum should move in any other direction, then you must take the time to go back and program your pendulum again.

- *Show me the direction that represents **not sure**.*

Stay focused on this statement until your pendulum moves in the direction that represents not sure. If your pendulum should move in any other direction, then you must take the time to go back and program your pendulum again.

Test 2:

Ask two or three questions where your Pendulum will answer either Yes or No. Be sure you know the answer with certainty.

Examples of possible testing questions may include:

- *Is my name _____?*
- *Is my address _____?*
- *Is my age _____?*

If the answers are not correct, go back and repeat the programing of yes and no until the test works out positively.

9- Subconscious Commitment

To establish a subconscious commitment, ask your pendulum the following questions:

- *My intention with using this pendulum is to help myself in a positive and healthy way. Does my subconscious mind understand my positive intention?*

- *To achieve the best possible results with the pendulum I need the full cooperation of my subconscious mind. Is my subconscious mind willing to work with me to achieve the best possible results?*

- *In this exercise I want to let go of ___ (state a specific negative emotion) totally and completely, in a healthy and safe way. Is my subconscious mind willing to work with me to let go of ___ in a healthy and safe way?*

Only continue if your subconscious mind responds yes to each of these questions.

10- Program Your Pendulum for Scale or Range

Using the Scale or Range Pendulum Chart at the back of the book will help with focus.

- Swing the pendulum forwards and back in the direction of **"0"** on your Scale or Range Pendulum Chart as you repeat:

This is the direction to represent "0" (or Low) with my subconscious mind. (3 times)

Stop your pendulum and again hold it directly above black dot that represents the **starting point.**

- This time swing the pendulum forwards and back in the direction of **"100"** on your Scale or Range Pendulum Chart as you repeat:

This is the direction to represent "100" (or High) with my subconscious mind. (3 times)

11- Test the Programing

Now ask your pendulum to show you specific directions as a test.

- Show me the direction for Low.
- Show me the direction for High.

If the signals are not correct, go back repeat the programing of a **scale** until the test works out positively.

12- Current Vibrational Frequency

Ask your Pendulum to use the scale to show you your current vibrational frequency.

13- Increasing Your Vibrational Frequency

As your pendulum moves to indicate your current vibrational frequency, direct your subconscious mind to increase your vibrational frequency so that the Law of Attraction will work better for you.

Direct your Subconscious Mind to increase your vibrational frequency by repeating the following statement over and over.

With every breath I take my subconscious mind increases my vibrational Frequency, in a healthy and safe way, so that the Law of Attraction will work better for me.

If the answer is **not clear,** ask your pendulum to show you a more clear and easier to see answer.

Notice that the pendulum starts to move towards "100" as your subconscious mind increases your vibrational frequency.

14- Clear the Pendulum

After you feel that you have increased your vibrational frequency to a more comfortable level, it is time to **clear your pendulum.**

Hold the weight of your pendulum in the palm of your other hand. This will relax the energy in your pendulum and allow it to prepare for the next question.

15- Say Thank You to Your Pendulum

While you are holding the weight of your Pendulum in your hands, say *thank you to your Pendulum for allowing you to experience all the benefits of the exercise.* .

16- Say Thank You to Your Subconscious Mind

While continuing to hold the weight of your Pendulum in your hands, say *thank you* to your subconscious mind for allowing you to experience all the benefits of this exercise.

17- Back to Full Awareness

After you say thank you to your subconscious mind, you can take a deep breath and bring yourself back to full awareness.

Communication with your Spirit Guides

Communication with Spirit Guides

In this exercise, we will start by using our **Yes – No** Pendulum Chart to create a connection with our Subconscious Mind, then we will use our **Yes – No** Pendulum Chart again to create a second connection with our Spirit Guide. Our Spirit Guide will be able to answer our "Yes" or "No" questions from the perspective of the Spirit World.

1- Get Emotionally Ready

Take several slow deep breaths and allow yourself to relax before you begin the exercise.

2- Get Mentally Ready

Take a deep breath and allow yourself to relax. Clear your mind of all chatter and focus all your attention on the Pendulum exercise you are about to work through. The more mentally relaxed you feel while using your Pendulum, the stronger the results you will experience.

3- Get Physically Ready

Find a comfortable place where you feel relaxed and at ease. Ideally, you should sit up straight, with both feet flat on the floor. Hold the string or chain of your pendulum between your thumb and forefinger of the hand that you write with. There should be at least 2 or 3 inches between your fingers and the pendulum. Be sure that your arm and elbow are not resting on anything.

4- Set Your Intention

In order for you to receive guidance from your Spirit Guides, you must set your intention by holding your Pendulum in both hands as you say:

My intention with this exercise is to receive positive and helpful guidance from my Spirit Guides.

5- Focus Your Energy

Now allow your Pendulum to hang free. It should be still as you allow it to hang there.

Focus your attention on your Pendulum. Stare at your Pendulum. Place all your concentration on your pendulum.

Allow yourself to be aware of your Pendulum Chart through your peripheral vision as you hold your full attention on your Pendulum.

6- Connecting with Your Subconscious Mind

Take a deep breath and allow yourself to relax. Ask your Pendulum to move in some way as an indication you are connected to your subconscious mind. Be patient and wait for your Pendulum to move as the sign you are connected to your subconscious mind.

7- Program Your Pendulum for Your Subconscious Mind

- Hold your pendulum so that it is hanging about two inches above the direct center of your **Yes or No Pendulum Chart.**

- Swing the pendulum forwards and back as you repeat the following statement three times:

*This is the direction to represent **Yes** with my subconscious mind. (3 times)*

- Swing the pendulum from left to right as you repeat three times:

*This is the direction to represent **No** with my subconscious mind. (3 times)*

- Swing the pendulum on an angle from top right to bottom left as you repeat three times:

*This is the direction to represent **Maybe** with my subconscious mind. (3 times)*

- Swing the Pendulum on an angle from top left to bottom right as you repeat three times:

*This is the direction to represent **Rephrase Question** with my subconscious mind. (3 times)*

8- Test the Programing

Test 1:

Focus all your attention on the pendulum as you repeat the following statements one at a time:

- *Show me the direction that represents **yes**.*

Stay focused on this statement until your pendulum moves in the direction that represents yes. If your pendulum should move in any other direction, then you must take the time to go back and program your pendulum again.

- *Show me the direction that represents **no**.*

Stay focused on this statement until your pendulum moves in the direction that represents no. If your pendulum should move in any other direction, then you must take the time to go back and program your pendulum again.

- *Show me the direction that represents **maybe**.*

Stay focused on this statement until your pendulum moves in the direction that represents maybe. If your pendulum should move in any other direction, then you must take the time to go back and program your pendulum again.

- *Show me the direction that represents **not sure**.*

Stay focused on this statement until your pendulum moves in the direction that represents not sure. If your pendulum should move in any other direction, then you must take the time to go back and program your pendulum again.

Test 2:

Ask two or three questions where your Pendulum will answer either Yes or No. Be sure you know the answer with certainty.

Examples of possible testing questions may include:

- *Is my name _____?*
- *Is my address _____?*
- *Is my age _____?*

If the answers are not correct, go back and repeat the programming of yes and no until the test works out positively.

9- Subconscious Commitment

To establish a subconscious commitment, ask your pendulum the following questions:

- *My intention with using this pendulum is to help myself in a positive and healthy way. Does my subconscious mind understand my positive intention?*

- *To achieve the best possible results with the pendulum I need the full cooperation of my subconscious mind. Is my subconscious mind willing to work with me to achieve the best possible results?*

- *In this exercise I want to let go of ____ (state a specific negative emotion) totally and completely, in a healthy and safe way. Is my* *subconscious mind willing to work with me to let go of ___ in a healthy and safe way?*

Only continue if your subconscious mind responds yes to each of these questions.

10- Connecting with your Spirit Guide

At this point we want to move from a connection with the subconscious mind to a higher connection. This higher connection is your connection with your Spirit Guide.

To connect with your Spirit Guide, continue to breathe easily, and allow yourself to relax even more. Ask your pendulum to move in some way as an indication you are connected to your Higher Conscious.

11- Program Your Pendulum for Communication with your Spirit Guide

Once your pendulum has moved to indicate a connection with your

Spirit Guide, you now need to program your pendulum so that you can communicate.

- Hold your pendulum so that it is hanging about two inches above the direct center of your **Yes or No Pendulum Chart.**

- Swing the pendulum forwards and back as you repeat the following statement three times:

*This is the direction to represent **Yes** with my Spirit Guide. (3 times)*

- Swing the pendulum from left to right as you repeat three times:

*This is the direction to represent **No** with my Spirit Guide. (3 times)*

- Swing the pendulum on an angle from top right to bottom left as you repeat three times:

*This is the direction to represent **Maybe** with my Spirit Guide. (3 times)*

- Swing the Pendulum on an angle from top left to bottom right as you repeat three times:

*This is the direction to represent **Rephrase Question** with my Spirit Guide. (3 times)*

12- Test the Programing

Test 1:

Focus all your attention on the pendulum as you repeat the following statements one at a time:

- *Show me the direction that represents **yes**.*

Stay focused on this statement until your pendulum moves in the direction that represents yes. If your pendulum should move in any other direction, then you must take the time to go back and program your pendulum again.

- *Show me the direction that represents **no**.*

Stay focused on this statement until your pendulum moves in the direction that represents no. If your pendulum should move in any other direction, then you must take the time to go back and program your pendulum again.

- *Show me the direction that represents **maybe**.*

Stay focused on this statement until your pendulum moves in the direction that represents maybe. If your pendulum should move in any other direction, then you must take the time to go back and program your pendulum again.

- *Show me the direction that represents **not sure**.*

Stay focused on this statement until your pendulum moves in the direction that represents not sure. If your pendulum should move in any other direction, then you must take the time to go back and program your pendulum again.

Test 2:

Ask two or three questions where your Pendulum will answer either Yes or No. Be sure you know the answer with certainty.

Examples of possible testing questions may include:

- *Is my name _____?*
- *Is my address _____?*
- *Is my age _____?*

If the answers are not correct, go back and repeat the programing of yes and no until the test works out positively.

13- Spirit Guide Commitment

To establish a higher level commitment, ask your pendulum the following questions:

- *My intention with using this pendulum is to help myself in a positive and healthy way. Does my Spirit Guide understand my positive intention?*

- *To achieve the best possible results with the pendulum I need the full cooperation of my Spirit Guide. Is my Spirit Guide willing to work with me to achieve the best possible results?*

- *In this exercise I want to receive answers to some very specific questions. Is my Spirit Guide willing to work with me by providing the answers that will serve me in the best possible way?*

Only continue if your Spirit Guide responds yes to each of these questions.

14- Asking Yes or No Questions

Questions should be clear and understandable and should always lead to a **yes** or **no** answer. Questions should only be about you.

Be sure that your pendulum comes to a complete stop between questions so that nothing can influence the answer to the next question.

If the answer is not clear, ask your pendulum to show you a more clear and easier to see answer.

15- Saying Thank You After Each Answer

It is important to say *thank you* after you receive an answer to each of your questions. This will keep you in a positive frame of mind where the focus is gratitude.

16- Say Thank You to Your Spirit Guide

When you have finished asking all your questions, say thank you to your Spirit Guide for all the help and guidance you have received.

17- Clear the Pendulum

After you have said thank you to your Spirit Guide, it is important that you **clear your pendulum** so that it is clear that you are finished with that question and you are ready to end the exercise.

To clear your pendulum, simply hold the weight of your pendulum in the palm of your hand. This will relax the energy in your pendulum and allow you to end the session.

15- Say Thank You to Your Pendulum

While you are holding the weight of your Pendulum in your hands, say *thank you to your Pendulum for allowing you to experience all the benefits of the exercise.* .

16- Say Thank You to Your Subconscious Mind

While continuing to hold the weight of your Pendulum in your hands, say *thank you* to your subconscious mind for allowing you to experience all the benefits of this exercise.

20- Back to Full Awareness

After you say *thank you* to your subconscious mind, you can take a deep breath and bring yourself back to full awareness.

Pendulum Charts

226 The Pendulum

Practice Pendulum Chart

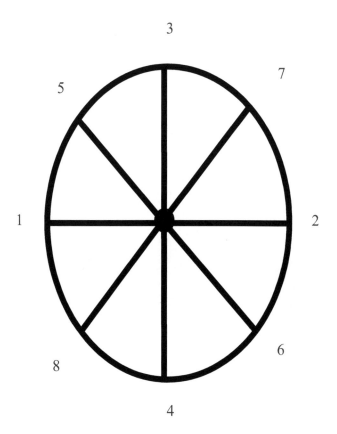

228 The Pendulum

Yes or No Pendulum Chart

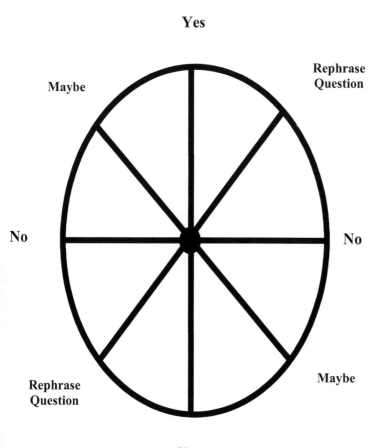

230 The Pendulum

Scale or Range

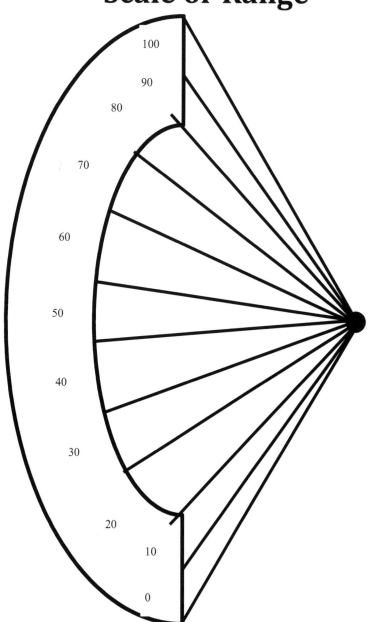

232 The Pendulum

Low – High Scale

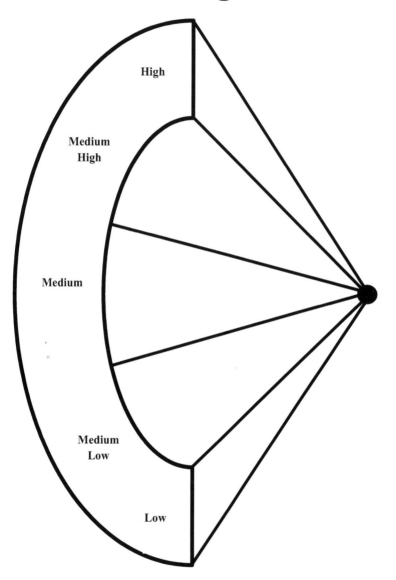

234 The Pendulum

Abundance – Scarcity Scale

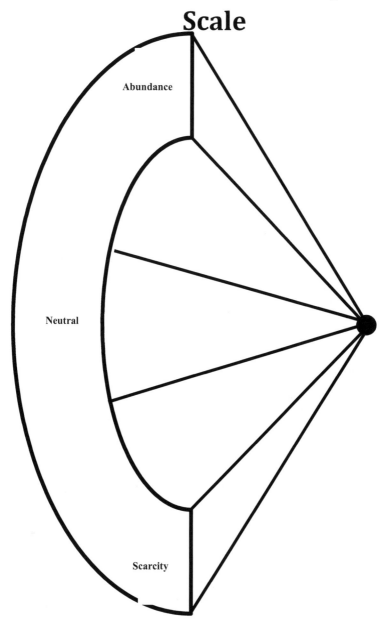

The Pendulum 237
Relaxed – Stressed Scale

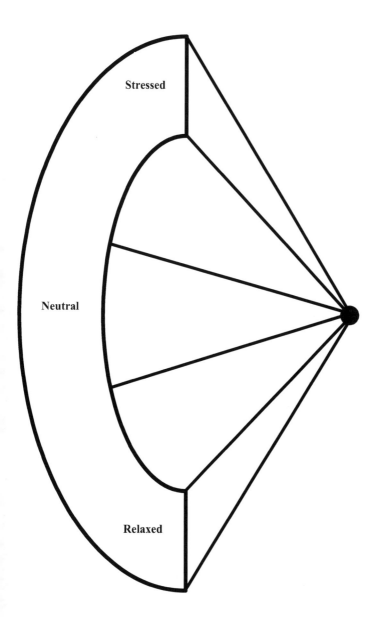

The Pendulum 239
Vibrational Frequency

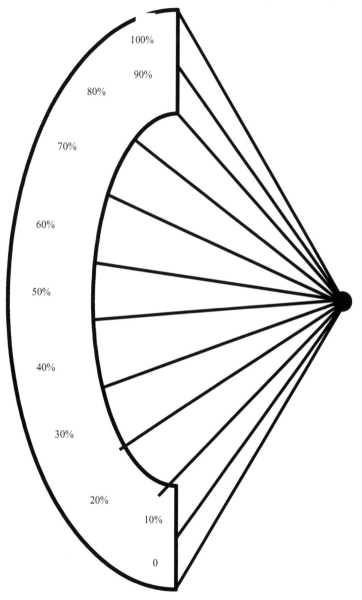

240 The Pendulum

Personal Power

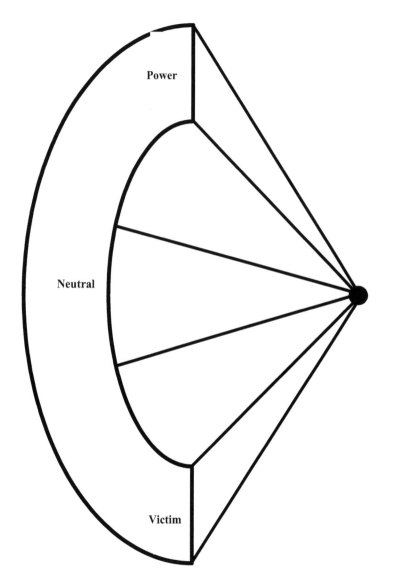

21 Day Challenge

21 Day Challenge

It takes 21 Days to create a new habit. Taking the 21 Day Challenge will allow you to become more comfortable using your pendulum and to get into the habit of using your pendulum on a regular basis.

Days 1 and 2
Select a pendulum that you feel comfortable with. Create a connection with your pendulum by allowing your energy and the energy of the pendulum to get in line. Carry your pendulum with you. Hold it often. Sleep with your pendulum under your pillow. Allow your pendulum to take on your energy

Day 3
Work through your pendulum practice exercises until you feel comfortable using the pendulum and are able to move the pendulum in all directions.

Days 4 to 6
Once you feel comfortable that your energy and the energy of your pendulum

are in alignment, it is time to move on to using your pendulum.

Now you want to get comfortable with programing your pendulum and asking simple questions that you already know the answers to. This will allow you to build your confidence with your pendulum and help you to better interpret the information you are receiving from your pendulum.

Days 7 to 10
The focus for this period is to become comfortable asking **yes** or **no** questions that you do not know the answers to.

Days 11 to 14
The focus for this period is to become comfortable asking **range** questions that you do not know the answers to.

Days 15 to 20

As you become more comfortable with using your pendulum, you can start working through the different applications of the pendulum present in this book.

Do one application each day to help you get more comfortable.

Day 21

Now that you are comfortable with your pendulum, it is time to start applying your new skills in all areas of your life.

Be patient and have fun as you become more and more confident with the use of your pendulum.

Printed in Poland
by Amazon Fulfillment
Poland Sp. z o.o., Wrocław